winter
warmers

Over 60 warming recipes, low in points...

WENDY VEALE

SIMON & SCHUSTER
A VIACOM COMPANY

Published in Great Britain by Simon & Schuster UK Ltd, 2000.
A Viacom Company.

Copyright © 2000, Weight Watchers International, Inc.

First published 2001
Reprinted 2003

Simon & Schuster UK Ltd.
Africa House
64–78 Kingsway
London WC2B 6AH

Weight Watchers and Pure Points are Trademarks of
Weight Watchers International, Inc. and used under its
control by Weight Watchers (UK) Ltd.

Photography: Steve Baxter
Styling: Marian Price
Food preparation: Joy Skipper
Design: Jane Humphrey
Typesetting: Stylize Digital Artwork
Printed and bound in China

Weight Watchers Publications Manager: Elizabeth Egan
Weight Watchers Publications Executive: Corrina Griffin
Weight Watchers Publications Assistant: Celia Whiston

A CIP catalogue record for this book is available
from the British Library

ISBN 0 743 23942 3

Pictured on the front cover: Beef in Beer with Dumplings (page 27)
Pictured on the back cover: Chicken Hotpot (page 15)

❶ denotes a vegetarian recipe and where relevant assumes that vegetarian cheese and
free-range eggs are used.

contents

4 Introduction

7 Satisfying Soups

15 Fabulous Fish & Poultry

22 Hot Hits with Meat

31 Vital Veggies

38 Hearty Puds & Desserts

49 Teatime Treats

55 Festive Fun

64 Index

While we all realise that the global climate is changing, bringing about elements of surprise in the weather, one thing that does not seem to change with it are our eating habits! Our glorious (if sometimes too wet) seasons bring with them spring – with plentiful new, fresh young produce which entices us into summer eating 'al fresco-style', healthy, casual and carefree. Then along comes harvest time, regarded by many as a new start to the year ahead – new careers or schools for the children with holidays now behind us; autumn produce finds its way into the local markets and shops, nights draw in as we all gasp at the early signs of Christmas as it makes its way into the shops before Guy Fawkes has hit the bonfire! Many people do not look forward to this change in seasons, but perhaps more so those of us who want to maintain those easier, hazy ways of summer – with foods that fit in so readily with **pure points**™.

healthy and warming
winter food

Then, as the weather changes again, we see the onset of winter. This book is here to help you welcome in the warming, wintery food that we nostalgically hanker after! Comfort food at its best but without too much fat – steaming puddings, simmering stews and bubbling bakes to enjoy with family or friends after work, thick soups and hearty broths to see you through the day at home or away, and to help keep colds and chills at bay. Enjoy the weekend treat of snuggling up on the sofa with a mug of hot tea and a delicious slice of cake, or ending the day with family or friends, enjoying a traditional hotpot – the heavenly cooking smells having lured you in from the cold on more than one occasion! It was worth waiting for... Relax and enjoy these times and the wonderful home cooking these darker months encourage. **pure points**™ is helping you to keep plenty of sunshine in your life so that you are on target to step out of those winter woollies into the brighter, lighter days ahead.

HOT HINTS AND TIPS

● Always have a bowl of low Point or no Point home-made soup handy in the refrigerator or freezer. The colder weather encourages us to eat more, so make sure you are prepared with tasty low Point treats ready to be heated up.

● Invest in a wide-rimmed thermos flask for those chunkier thick soups and winter stews – great for seeing you through the day if you are out and about or at work.

● Stock up on plenty of zero Point vegetables to bulk out meals and to keep your winter appetite satisfied.

● Plan your weekly shopping to ensure you have the time and ingredients to cook your favourite dishes. Remember that many of the recipes in this book, particularly the casseroles and bakes, will reheat well, and often taste better a day or two after cooking. Batch bake and freeze portions where possible.

● Invest in some small ramekin dishes or pudding basins. If you only require one or two servings, they will make it easier to store the additional portions either in the freezer or fridge for another occasion.

● At least twice a year take stock of your store cupboards – throw out old ingredients which are beyond their 'best before' date. Stock up on different spices, dried fruits and baking goods so that you have them to hand for the season ahead. Enjoy the prospect of new flavours!

● If you have one, learn how to use the automatic timer on your oven.

This will help you plan meals which are ready and waiting for you to come home to. Have a practice run when you are at home to check the timing of the cooking. An electric slow cooker is a terrific investment for cooking over the winter months – perfect for soups, steamed puddings and casseroles, and also for keeping food warm over a period of time (but check in the manufacturer's handbook for recommended temperatures and times).

● For special and festive occasions, the key word – again – is 'Plan'! Do not get caught out – allow yourself enough time to prepare food which fits in with *pure points*™. You will find lots of suitable recipes in Teatime Treats (page 49). Make sure you have some Point free nibbles to munch on.

● Fresh meat or vegetable stocks are far superior to the powdered or cube variety. They freeze well too, so have a quantity handy for adding to soups, stews and casseroles. They really are worth it – nearly as good as homemade!

● Steaming is the healthiest method of cooking. Not only is it quick but also, when cooking vegetables and fruit, it preserves a higher proportion of nutrients than other conventional methods. The flavours and textures of all steamed food are superb too. You will find that most steaming recipes are naturally low in fat, which has to be good!

● And finally… relax and make the most of the variety of seasonal dishes available to you. As you learn to change your way of eating for life, there is no need to miss out on one of life's pleasures – good homely food!

Golden Onion Soup: Fabulous with a low-fat cheese-topped slice of bread for only 5½ Points per serving.

Comforting, warming and nourishing – a bowl of steaming hot soup on a bitterly cold day will have you 'souped up' in no time at all, ready to face the next challenge of the day!

Soup is a great 'stop-gap' when you are feeling peckish. It is easy to transport in a thermos flask for a satisfying snack away from home – and while we all have our favourite ' stand-bys' handy in the store cupboard, why not enjoy the fresh flavours and low Points of these delicious seasonal recipes? Make up a batch to freeze for the cold winter months, saving some in the refrigerator, for use over several days at a time, to heat you up and warm you right through.

GOLDEN ONION SOUP

POINTS

per recipe: 2¹/₂   per serving: ¹/₂

Ⓥ *Serves 6*
Preparation time: 10 minutes
Cooking time: 35 minutes
Freezing: recommended
Calories per serving: 60

Throughout history, onions have been revered as a natural cure or preventative for many ailments! Whether an old wives' tale or not, they are a principal ingredient in cooking so let's hope they are doing us some good – my mother used to encourage me to eat roast onions when I had a cold! Make a batch of this delicious low Point soup to keep any sort of chill at bay!

low-fat cooking spray
600 g (1 lb 5 oz) onions, halved and sliced finely
1 teaspoon granulated sugar
1 potato (approximately 175 g/6 oz), diced
1.2 litres (2 pints) hot vegetable or chicken stock
1 tablespoon chopped fresh thyme, plus extra sprigs to garnish (or 1 teaspoon dried)
salt and freshly ground black pepper

1 Spray a non-stick saucepan with the low-fat cooking spray, toss in the onions and sugar, and cook over a low heat for 12–15 minutes, stirring frequently, until the onions are golden.

2 Add the potato, half the stock and thyme. Season with a little salt and pepper and bring to simmering point. Cover and cook for 15 minutes or until the potato is tender.

3 Use a slotted spoon to remove some of the cooked onions for a nice texture if desired and then liquidise the remaining soup until smooth. Return the reserved onions to the saucepan if relevant, and the remaining thyme. Adjust the seasoning to taste.

4 Serve the soup garnished with extra sprigs of thyme if using fresh.

TOP TIP Take your time to cook the onions carefully and slowly at step 1, as the natural sugars in the onions will slowly caramelise.

VARIATION For a main meal soup, serve each portion of soup topped with 2 tablespoons half-fat grated Cheddar cheese and a 1-inch (2.5 cm) slice of French bread. Add 3 Points per serving.

If you prefer, replace the thyme with snipped fresh chives.

1 Spray a non-stick saucepan with the low-fat cooking spray. Add the onion, garlic and beetroot. Cover and cook gently for 10 minutes, shaking the pan occasionally.

2 Add the tomatoes, tomato juice, purée, spices and stock. Cover and bring to the boil. Reduce the heat and simmer gently for 15 minutes or until the vegetables are tender. Season well.

3 Purée in a liquidiser until very smooth. Adjust the seasoning to taste. Reheat gently and ladle into warmed bowls. Garnish with a tablespoon of yogurt and a drizzle of soy sauce.

TOP TIPS To skin fresh tomatoes, put them in a bowl and cover with boiling water for a few minutes, then drain and leave to cool slightly. Use a small knife to peel off the skin which should come away from the flesh easily.

For added convenience, replace the fresh tomatoes and tomato juice with a 400 g can of chopped tomatoes.

VARIATION For a fruity note, add 1 medium cooking apple, peeled, cored and chopped, at step 2. Core and finely slice a red-skinned dessert apple to garnish the soup too. Add ½ Point per serving.

Red Hot Tomato and Beetroot Soup: Beetroot and tomato are a dynamic taste combination. Try it!

RED HOT TOMATO AND BEETROOT SOUP

POINTS

per recipe: 1   per serving: 0

Ⓥ Serves 4
Preparation time: 10 minutes
Cooking time: 30 minutes
Calories per serving: 65
Freezing: recommended

A delicious blend of tomatoes and beetroot 'warmed up' with a hint of cumin, this seasonal soup makes you glow just by looking at it! It looks attractive, too, served with a swirl of low-fat plain yogurt. Perfect for entertaining.

low-fat cooking spray
1 large onion, chopped
1 garlic clove, crushed
225 g (8 oz) raw beetroot, grated or finely sliced
225 g (8 oz) fresh tomatoes, skinned and roughly chopped
300 ml (½ pint) tomato juice
1 tablespoon tomato purée
1 teaspoon ground cumin
½ teaspoon ground cinnamon
600 ml (1 pint) hot vegetable stock
salt and freshly ground black pepper
4 tablespoons low-fat plain yogurt
soy sauce, to drizzle

FARMHOUSE CHICKEN AND VEGETABLE BROTH

POINTS

per recipe: **23**   per serving: **5½**

Serves 4
Preparation time: 10 minutes
Cooking time: 1 hour
Calories per serving: 270
Freezing: recommended

Bring back nostalgia and enjoy this mighty main meal soup with the family for a mid-week supper or Saturday lunch. Little else is needed except a healthy appetite!

low-fat cooking spray

1 large onion, sliced finely

2 large carrots, cut into 1 cm (½-inch) slices

2 sticks celery, sliced

250 g (9 oz) swede, cut into chunks

65 g (2½ oz) pearl barley

500 g (1 lb 2 oz) chicken thighs, skinless but on the bone

1.5 litres (2¾ pints) hot chicken or vegetable stock

350 g (12 oz) mushrooms, sliced thickly

1 teaspoon dried sage (or 1 tablespoon finely chopped fresh)

2 tablespoons cornflour

2 teaspoons Worcestershire sauce

2 tablespoons fresh chopped parsley

salt and freshly ground black pepper

1 Spray a large casserole dish or saucepan with low-fat cooking spray. Stir-fry the onion, carrots, celery and swede for 5 minutes until slightly softened. Add the pearl barley and the chicken pieces. Continue to stir-fry for 3–4 minutes, or until the chicken is lightly coloured.

2 Add the stock and bring to the boil, then lower the heat, cover and simmer gently for 35–40 minutes.

(During this time the barley will swell and soften, absorbing some of the stock.)

3 Use tongs to remove the cooked chicken to a chopping board. Add the mushrooms and sage to the saucepan, and continue to simmer, uncovered, for 10 minutes. Meanwhile, remove the chicken from the bones and roughly shred. Return the meat to the saucepan. Season well, to taste.

4 Blend the cornflour to a paste with the Worcestershire sauce and a drop of cold water. Stir into the broth and continue to heat through until the broth thickens slightly. Check the seasoning.

5 Ladle into warm bowls, scatter on the parsley and serve immediately.

TOP TIPS Choose chicken thighs or legs for the best flavour and succulence.

Dark-gilled open mushrooms will add more flavour and depth to this broth than button mushrooms, so look out for those.

Farmhouse Chicken and Vegetable Broth: A hearty and satisfying main meal soup.

FISHERMAN'S CATCH

POINTS

per recipe: 13½   per serving: 3½

Serves 4
Preparation time: 10 minutes
Cooking time: 25 minutes
Calories per serving: 260
Freezing: not recommended

Look out for any bargain non-oily fish like haddock or cod, and for added flavour, include some smoked fish. A handful of cooked prawns and mussels add a touch of luxury, adjusting the Points as necessary.

350 g (12 oz) skinless fish fillets, i.e. cod, whiting or haddock

225 g (8 oz) potatoes, peeled and cut into 1 cm (½-inch) dice

2 medium leeks or onions, sliced

175 g (6 oz) carrots, coarsely grated

100 g (3½ oz) frozen peas

2 tablespoons cornflour

600 ml (1 pint) semi-skimmed milk

salt and freshly ground black pepper

snipped fresh chives or chopped fresh parsley, to garnish

1 Simmer the fish in 600 ml (1 pint) of water for 10 minutes, until tender. Drain, reserving the liquid. Flake the fish coarsely, discarding any skin and bones.

2 Return the strained cooking liquid to the pan. Add the potatoes, leeks or onions and carrots and simmer, covered, for 10 minutes or until the vegetables are tender. Add the peas.

3 Blend the cornflour with enough milk to make a smooth paste. Stir into the saucepan and bring to a steady boil, stirring continuously until the soup thickens. Stir in the remaining milk.

4 Season with a little salt and plenty of freshly ground black pepper. Serve in warmed bowls, garnished with the fresh herbs.

TOP TIPS Let your fishmonger know what you are cooking. There may be some tail end pieces and odds and ends of assorted fish which can be used up in a chowder – at a very much reduced price!

This soup is a substantial meal in itself, and ideal for a warming thermos flask lunch.

VARIATIONS Add a teaspoon of curry paste at step 2 for a Spicy Fish Soup. This will add no Points per serving.

If you have more Points to spare, swirl 1 tablespoon of single cream into each soup bowl just before serving. Add 1 Point per serving. Replace the peas with 100 g (3½ oz) baby leaf spinach.

SPICED TOMATO, LENTIL AND RICE SOUP

POINTS

per recipe: 9½   per serving: 2½

 Serves 4
Preparation time: 10 minutes
Cooking time: 35 minutes
Calories per serving: 180
Freezing: recommended

Serve as a main meal soup with a medium, toasted pitta bread. Add 2½ Points per serving

100 g (3½ oz) dried red lentils, rinsed and drained

400 g can chopped tomatoes

1 tablespoon tomato purée

3 celery sticks, chopped

2 medium carrots, coarsely grated

1.2 litres (2 pints) hot vegetable stock

50 g (1¾ oz) long-grain rice

1 tablespoon vegetable oil

1 large onion, chopped

1 tablespoon fresh chopped ginger (or 1 teaspoon ground)

2 teaspoons ground coriander

1 teaspoon ground cumin

½ teaspoon hot chilli powder

½ teaspoon turmeric

4 tablespoons low-fat plain yogurt

salt and freshly ground black pepper

1 Place the dried lentils, tomatoes, purée, celery, carrots and stock in a saucepan, bring to the boil then cover and simmer for 10 minutes. Stir in the rice and simmer for a further 15 minutes.

2 Meanwhile, heat the oil in a small non-stick saucepan, and fry the onion until golden brown. Add the ginger, coriander, cumin and chilli powder and gently fry for 3–4 minutes. Stir in the turmeric.

3 Stir the spices into the soup. Simmer for 5 minutes and check the seasoning.

4 Serve piping hot topped with a tablespoon of yogurt.

TOP TIP It is important to first fry ground spices before adding to other ingredients. The heat will release their natural fragrant oils and prevent an otherwise slightly bitter aftertaste and chalky feel in the mouth.

VARIATION This soup liquidises well but you may need to adjust the consistency by adding hot stock.

Fisherman's Catch:
A simple, delicious
and filling chowder
for only 3½ Points.

POTATO AND CELERIAC SOUP

POINTS

per recipe: 4   per serving: 1

Ⓥ Serves 4

Preparation time: 10 minutes
Cooking time: 35 minutes
Calories per serving: 115
Freezing: recommended

A great way of ensuring you get your quota of greens!

low-fat cooking spray

350 g (12 oz) potatoes, peeled and cut into chunks

350 g (12 oz) celeriac, peeled and cut into chunks

1 large onion, chopped

1 garlic clove, crushed

1 green chilli, de-seeded and chopped finely (optional)

200 g (7 oz) winter greens (i.e. Savoy cabbage or green cabbage), shredded finely

1.2 litres (2 pints) hot vegetable stock

salt and freshly ground black pepper

1 Spray a large saucepan with the low-fat cooking spray and add the potatoes, celeriac, onion, garlic and chilli. Cover and cook over a gentle heat for 10 minutes, shaking the pan occasionally, until the vegetables have softened without colouring.

2 Meanwhile, plunge the shredded greens into a pan of lightly salted boiling water and cook for just 3–4 minutes until wilted. Drain and refresh the greens under cold running water then drain thoroughly. Set aside.

3 Add the stock to the vegetables, season with salt and pepper, bring up to simmering point and simmer gently, covered, for 20 minutes, or until the vegetables are very tender.

4 Liquidise the soup until smooth. Return to the saucepan together with the wilted greens and reheat gently. Check the seasoning before serving, piping hot.

TOP TIPS Choose your favourite winter greens for this recipe. Shredded Brussels sprouts and spinach are also delicious and full of flavour at this time of year.

Unless freezing, use the soup within a day or two of making as the celeriac does tend to discolour slightly.

VARIATIONS Omit the chilli if you prefer a milder level of heat – but be generous when adding freshly ground black pepper. Chicken stock gives a good depth of flavour for non-vegetarians.

HARVEST VEGETABLE SOUP

POINTS

per recipe: 11   per serving: 2½

Ⓥ Serves 4

Preparation time: 10 minutes
Cooking time: 45 minutes
Calories per serving: 245
Freezing: recommended

Store in the fridge, covered, for up to four days.

1 tablespoon olive oil

1 large onion, chopped

1 garlic clove, crushed

1 large leek, halved lengthwise and cut into 5 mm (¼-inch) slices

2 medium carrots, chopped into 1 cm (½-inch) dice

2 stalks celery, sliced (including the leafy tops)

1 medium potato (approximately 225 g/8 oz), quartered and cut into 5 mm (¼-inch) slices

3 heaped teaspoons vegetable bouillon powder or 1 vegetable stock cube

300 ml (½ pint) creamed tomato or passata

2 sprigs fresh thyme or oregano

400 g tin chick-peas, drained

⅛th Savoy cabbage, shredded

1 medium courgette, quartered lengthways and chopped

2 tablespoons chopped fresh parsley

salt and freshly ground black pepper

1 Heat the oil in a large saucepan, add the onion, garlic, leek, carrots, celery and potato. Cover and cook the vegetables over a gentle heat for 10 minutes, shaking the pan occasionally.

2 Pour 1.2 litres boiling water into a measuring jug. Add the bouillon powder or stock cube and stir until dissolved. Add the vegetable bouillon or stock cube, dissolved in a little water, creamed tomato or passata and fresh herbs. Cover and bring the soup to the boil, then simmer for 15 minutes.

3 Stir in the chick-peas, cabbage and courgette and simmer for a further 15 minutes. Season well with salt and freshly ground black pepper, and stir in the fresh parsley. The soup is now ready to ladle into warmed bowls and enjoy!

TOP TIP Marigold vegetable bouillon is now widely available in most supermarkets.

VARIATION Add 100 g (3½ oz) small soup pasta shapes at step 3 for a more substantial soup. Add 1½ Points per serving.

BUTTERBEAN AND BROCCOLI SOUP

POINTS

per recipe: 12   per serving: 3

Serves 4
Preparation time: 15 minutes
Cooking time: 20 minutes
Calories per serving: 160
Freezing: recommended

This is a truly satisfying soup – filling, tasty and packed full of nourishment to help keep the winter bugs at bay! Just 100 g (3½ oz) of boiled broccoli contains over half the recommended daily intake of Vitamin C.

Serve a generous bowlful with a medium slice of fresh crusty brown bread (1 Point). Great for the thermos flask too!

low-fat cooking spray

2 rashers, rindless smoked lean back bacon (about 25 g/1 oz each), chopped

1 large onion, chopped

1 garlic clove, crushed

400 g (14 oz) broccoli, roughly chopped

1.2 litres (2 pints) hot chicken or vegetable stock

2 × 420 g cans butterbeans, drained

1 teaspoon dried rosemary (or 1 tablespoon chopped fresh)

salt and freshly ground black pepper

1 Spray a large non-stick saucepan with the low-fat cooking spray and fry the bacon over a high heat until it is very crispy. Use a slotted spoon to transfer the bacon to a plate lined with absorbent kitchen paper. Set to one side.

2 Turn the heat down, add the onion, garlic and broccoli, cover and cook for 4–5 minutes or until softened, shaking the pan occasionally.

3 Pour in the stock and bring to the boil. Add the beans, rosemary, and the salt and pepper to taste, then cover and simmer for 15 minutes, until the broccoli is tender.

4 Liquidise two-thirds of the soup until smooth. Add the remaining third and liquidise for a short burst to coarsely chop the remaining vegetables. Return to the pan and reheat. Check the seasoning.

5 Ladle the soup into four warmed bowls and scatter on the crispy bacon bits. Serve immediately.

TOP TIP Choose broccoli that has good dark green florets – an indication of freshness and therefore higher nutritional value.

VARIATIONS To make this soup suitable for vegetarians, replace the chicken stock with vegetable stock and omit the bacon rashers. You will save 1 Point.

For a special garnish, sprinkle 1 teaspoon toasted flaked almonds over the soup. This will add ½ Point per serving.

Butterbean and Broccoli Soup: Only 3 Points per serving for a healthy bowl of warming soup.

QUICK GARNISHES

Treat yourself and your family to some quick yet low Point or no Point garnishes to add that finishing touch to a bowl of soup. Here are some ideas for you to enjoy!

Per serving:

1 tablespoon low-fat plain yogurt	**0 Points**
1 tablespoon half-fat crème fraîche	**½ Point**
1 tablespoon half-fat Cheddar cheese, grated	**½ Point**
1 teaspoon parmesan cheese, grated	**½ Point**
1 teaspoon chopped fresh herbs	**0 Points**
15 g (½ oz) sliced brown bread, toasted then cubed	**½ Point**
½ rasher lean bacon, grilled till crispy then crumbled	**½ Point**
1 teaspoon Worcestershire or soy sauce	**0 Points**
1 teaspoon toasted flaked almonds	**½ Point**

**Chicken Hotpot:
This comforting
casserole is
perfect for all
the family.**

Native fish and poultry are both at their prime during the colder months which means we are still able to enjoy their naturally low-fat content and nutritious qualities during the 'hungrier' months.

Here are some new, indulgent and tasty ways to enjoy winter warmth with these ingredients without compromising on Points or comfort around the waistband!

CHICKEN HOTPOT

POINTS

per recipe: 33½   per serving: 8½

Serves 4
Preparation time: 15 minutes
Cooking time: 1 hour 30 minutes
Calories per serving: 400
Freezing: recommended

'Hotpot' is a great description for this dish – healthy portions of wholesome yet simple ingredients cooked together over a gentle heat. This tasty dish will leave you with a warm glow – just right to set you up for a bracing afternoon walk!

4 skinless chicken legs, each approximately 200 g (7oz)
25 g (1 oz) seasoned flour
1 tablespoon vegetable oil
2 large carrots, cut into 2 cm (¾-inch) slices
3 sticks celery, sliced
125 g (4½ oz) green cabbage, shredded
2 medium leeks, trimmed and cut into 2 cm (¾-inch) slices
1 tablespoon chopped fresh thyme plus 1 teaspoon to garnish
2 baking potatoes, each approximately 300 g (10½ oz), cut into 5 mm (¼-inch) slices
425 ml (¾ pint) hot chicken or vegetable stock
2 teaspoons cornflour blended with a little cold water
salt and freshly ground black pepper

1 Preheat the oven to Gas Mark 5/ 190°C/375°F. Lightly dust the chicken joints with the seasoned flour. Heat the oil in a non-stick frying-pan, and sauté the chicken for 3–4 minutes, or until lightly browned on all sides.
2 Scatter half of the carrots, celery, cabbage and leeks over the base of a large casserole dish. Season and then continue to season as you layer.

Top with the chicken legs, scatter over the thyme and cover with the remaining vegetables. Overlap the potato slices on top of the vegetables.
3 Stir the hot stock into the blended cornflour until smooth. Gently pour over the casserole and cover lightly with a piece of foil, and cook in the oven for 1 hour.
4 Remove the foil, increase the oven temperature to Gas Mark 6/ 200°C/400°F, and cook for a further 25–30 minutes, until the potatoes are tender and golden. Serve, sprinkled with additional chopped fresh thyme.

VARIATION For a Lamb Hotpot, replace the chicken with 4 × 125 g (4½ oz) lean lamb loin chops or 8 boneless, skinless chicken thighs. Add these at step 2, and reduce the cooking time at step 3 to 30 minutes. Replace the thyme with rosemary. Points per serving will be 8.

1 Use a zester to remove the rind from the orange. Squeeze the juice into a bowl, add the zest, wine and the cinnamon stick or ground cinnamon.

2 Slice the chicken breasts across the grain, into 2.5 cm (1-inch) wide strips. Add to the orange mixture, coating the strips well. Cover and leave to marinate for 1 hour.

3 Place the onion, garlic, clove and saffron, if using, and tomatoes into a saucepan. Bring to the boil, then reduce the heat to a simmer, stir in the honey and leave the sauce to gently bubble for 20 minutes or until it thickens to a jam-like consistency.

4 Strain the chicken, reserving the marinade. Stir this into the sauce together with the Tabasco sauce. Season to taste.

5 Spray the low-fat cooking spray into a non-stick frying-pan and quickly brown the chicken all over. Add to the tomato sauce and simmer for a further 5 minutes. Now stir in the parsley and serve.

Chicken Casserole with Orange and Cinnamon: Flavourful and warming, with the wonderful tastes of the season.

CHICKEN CASSEROLE WITH ORANGE AND CINNAMON

POINTS

per recipe: 16   per serving: 4

Serves 4
Preparation time: 10 minutes + 1 hour marinating
Cooking time: 30 minutes
Calories per serving: 265
Freezing: recommended

Here is a great chicken recipe that has a ring of Christmas with ingredients such as oranges, cinnamon, cloves and honey. Make it several days in advance, both for convenience and also to allow the rich flavours to develop. Delicious with couscous and green beans but remember to add the Points.

1 large, juicy, sweet orange
4 tablespoons dry white wine
5 cm (2-inch) piece cinnamon stick or 1 level teaspoon ground cinnamon
4 skinless chicken breasts, each approximately 150 g (5½ oz)
1 large onion, chopped
1 garlic clove, crushed
1 clove (optional)
3–4 saffron strands (optional)
2 × 400 g cans chopped tomatoes
1 level tablespoon clear honey
a few dashes of Tabasco sauce
low-fat cooking spray
salt and freshly ground black pepper
1 tablespoon finely chopped parsley, to garnish

VARIATION This is also a great way of enjoying lamb in the winter months. Buy 400 g (14 oz) lean neck fillet (readily available in pre-pack form) and cut into thin slices. Cook at the beginning of step 5 for 5 minutes before adding to the sauce. Allow 100 g (3½ oz) lamb per person and 5½ Points per serving.

CHICKEN AND HAM PANCAKE PIE

POINTS

per recipe: 23½	per serving: 6

Serves 4
Preparation time: 15 minutes
Cooking time: 20 minutes
Calories per serving: 190
Freezing: recommended after step 4

Here is a clever, quick way to make a low-fat yet substantial 'pie' with a new twist: tasty pancake-lined ramekins, bubbling with a creamy traditional filling. Be sure to use the whole pack of pancake batter mix for thick, satisfying pancakes. Serve with carrots and broccoli.

---

127 g pack of pancake batter mix

1 medium egg

low-fat cooking spray

1 medium leek, sliced

2 × 150 g (5½ oz) skinless chicken breast, cut into 2 cm (¾-inch) pieces

450 g jar of Homepride 98% Fat-free Mushroom and Garlic Sauce

125 g (4½ oz) thick-sliced cooked ham, chopped

1 tablespoon chopped fresh chives

freshly ground black pepper

1 Preheat the oven to Gas Mark 5/180°C/375°F.

2 Make the pancake batter according to the packet instructions, adding the egg. Use low-fat cooking spray as required around the inside of a 20 cm (8-inch) non-stick omelette pan and make four pancakes.

3 Dry-fry the leek and chicken in a non-stick frying-pan for 5 minutes, or until the chicken has coloured. Stir in the mushroom sauce and ham, and heat through for 2 minutes. Season with freshly ground pepper then stir in the chives.

4 Line 4 × 10 cm (4-inch) bowls or ramekin dishes each with a pancake. Divide the chicken mixture between the ramekins, then fold in the overhanging pancakes to partly conceal the filling.

5 Cook for 15–20 minutes until the filling is bubbling and the edges are crispy. Serve immediately.

TOP TIP Make a batch of pancakes, wrap them individually in between layers of greaseproof paper and freeze them for up to 6 months. Simply remove one or two at a time as required. If freezing the pancakes filled (after step 4), cover and freeze for up to 6 weeks. Defrost thoroughly before continuing with the cooking instructions from step 5.

VARIATION For a vegetarian option, replace the chicken and ham with a small, lightly cooked cauliflower, broken into florets. Add to the leeks with the sauce at step 3. Sprinkle the top with 50 g (1¾ oz) grated half-fat vegetarian cheese at step 4. Allow 4 Points per serving.

Chicken and Ham Pancake Pie: You'll love delving into these satisfying pancakes!

TURKEY, PARSNIP AND CHEDDAR CRUMBLE

POINTS

per recipe: 32	per serving: 8

Serves 4
Preparation time: 30 minutes
Cooking time: 30 minutes
Calories per serving: 470
Freezing: recommended before baking
at step 5

This savoury surprise is delicious served with winter greens and chunky carrot slices.

350 g (12 oz) parsnip, cut into chunks
4 small leeks, cut into 2 cm (¾-inch) slices
low-fat cooking spray
350 g (12 oz) diced turkey
40 g (1½ oz) sauce flour
300 ml (½ pint) semi-skimmed milk
125 g (4½ oz) half-fat Cheddar cheese, grated finely
3 teaspoons Dijon or wholegrain mustard

FOR THE CRUMBLE TOPPING

100 g (3½ oz) plain flour
25 g (1 oz) low-fat spread (e.g. St. Ivel 'Gold')
50 g (1¾ oz) fresh breadcrumbs
1 tablespoon porridge oats
1 teaspoon chopped fresh rosemary or thyme
salt and freshly ground black pepper

1 Boil the parsnips for 5 minutes, then add the leeks and cook together for a further 8–10 minutes. Drain thoroughly, reserving 300 ml (½ pint) of the cooking water.
2 Spray a non-stick saucepan with the low-fat cooking spray, and stir-fry the turkey for 5 minutes, until lightly coloured. Sprinkle on the sauce flour, and gradually blend in the hot vegetable cooking water. Cook gently until smooth, then stir in the milk and 75 g (3 oz) cheese.
3 Fold in the cooked vegetables. Season to taste and add the mustard. Spoon the filling into a shallow ovenproof dish.

4 Preheat the oven to Gas Mark 5/ 190°C/375°F. To make the crumble, place the flour in a food processor bowl, add the low-fat spread and process until crumbly. Add the breadcrumbs and oats and process for a further second or so. Stir in the remaining cheese and the herbs.
5 Scatter the crumble over the vegetables, pressing down gently, then bake for 20–25 minutes until golden and bubbling. Serve immediately.

TOP TIP Sauce flour is now available in most supermarkets. It is ideal for blending into liquid without the need of added fat or the fear of a lumpy sauce. Keep a packet handy!

VARIATION For a tasty Prawn and Mushroom Crumble, replace the parsnip with equal quantities of carrot and broccoli, and replace the turkey with 225 g (8 oz) cooked peeled prawns and 125 g (4½ oz) button mushrooms, sliced. Points per serving will be the same.

STIR-FRY PRAWN CURRY

POINTS

per recipe: 4	per serving: 2

Serves 2
Preparation time: 10 minutes
Cooking time: 5 minutes
Calories per serving: 195
Freezing: not recommended

Serve on a bed of rice, noodles or some fresh steamed vegetables, adding the extra Points.

225 g (8 oz) cooked tiger prawns
1 tablespoon dry sherry
2 teaspoons light soy sauce
2 teaspoons vegetable or groundnut oil

1 small onion, roughly chopped
1 garlic clove, crushed
1 small fresh red or green chilli, de-seeded and chopped
1 teaspoon finely chopped fresh root ginger
1 stalk lemon grass, outer layer discarded and finely chopped
1 teaspoon Madras curry paste
½ teaspoon caster sugar
fresh coriander sprigs, to garnish

1 In a bowl, mix together the prawns, sherry and soy sauce. Cover and leave in a cool place until required. (This can be done several hours before they are needed.)
2 Heat the oil in a large frying-pan or wok and stir-fry the onion for 1 minute. Add the garlic, chilli, ginger, lemon grass and curry paste and stir-fry for a further minute
3 Add the prawns, soy sauce and sherry together with the sugar and 2 tablespoons of water. Stir-fry for 2 minutes, and serve immediately, garnished with the coriander.

TOP TIP Fresh chillies contain oils which can make sensitive skin tingle and eyes smart so rub your hands with a light coating of cooking oil, which will form a barrier. This makes it easier to wash off these hot oils.

VARIATION Replace the prawns with 250 g (9 oz) stir-fry strips of chicken, for 3½ Points per serving.

Stir-fry Prawn Curry: This quick curry will warm up friends and family in no time at all! With a medium portion of noodles, the Points per serving will be 5.

1 Heat the oil in a large saucepan and cook the onion and celery gently for 5 minutes. Stir in the garlic and spices, and cook for a further minute.

2 Stir in the chopped tomatoes, 150 ml (¼ pint) of water, and the purée. Bring to a steady boil, and stir in the rice. Reduce the heat, cover and simmer gently for 15 minutes.

3 Add the fish and chick-peas and season to taste. Cover and simmer for a further 10 minutes, until the fish is cooked. Stir in the chopped coriander, reserving a little to scatter over the top. Divide the casserole between four warmed plates, and top each with a spoonful of yogurt and a scattering of coriander. Serve immediately.

TOP TIP Habit often leads us to add the garlic at the same time as the onion in a recipe. Garlic can burn very quickly and become bitter tasting, so add it just as the onions are turning golden and soft.

VARIATION Replace the fish with 450 g (1 lb) skinless chicken thighs, adding them at step 1 with the spices. Stir-fry until lightly coloured, then proceed to step 2. This will be 6 Points per serving.

Spicy Fish Casserole: Chunky fish with fabulous spices make this a filling and tasty mid-week meal.

SPICY FISH CASSEROLE

POINTS

per recipe: 16   per serving: 4

Serves 4
Preparation time: 10 minutes
Cooking time: 35 minutes
Calories per serving: 320
Freezing: recommended

There's no need to neglect fish during the colder months – it is readily available and often at its best. While lighter than meat, fish is equally nutritious and satisfying. Try this great mid-week supper – chunky fish, chick-peas and rice, fragrantly warmed with spices and coriander. All that is required is a bowlful of fresh green vegetables and a healthy appetite!

1 tablespoon vegetable oil
1 medium onion, chopped
3 sticks celery, finely chopped
1 garlic clove, crushed
2 teaspoons ground cumin
1 teaspoon paprika
2 × 400 g cans chopped tomatoes
1 tablespoon tomato purée
50 g (1¾ oz) long-grain rice
500 g (1 lb 2 oz) skinless thick cod fillet, cut into 4 cm (1½-inch) cubes
1 × 400 g can chick-peas, drained and rinsed
3 tablespoons chopped fresh coriander
4 tablespoons low-fat plain yogurt
salt and freshly ground black pepper

FISH PIE

POINTS

per recipe: $21\frac{1}{2}$ per serving: $5\frac{1}{2}$

Serves 4
Preparation time: 15 minutes
Cooking time: 30 minutes
Calories per serving: 360
Freezing: recommended

Serve this pie bubbling hot straight from the oven, with green vegetables and ripe beef tomatoes, baked alongside the pie.

1 medium onion, chopped
1 stick celery, sliced
1 medium red pepper, de-seeded, quartered and cut into strips
1 tablespoon vegetable oil
450 ml ($\frac{3}{4}$ pint) semi-skimmed milk
2 tablespoons cornflour
2 tablespoons chopped fresh parsley
1 tablespoon lemon or lime juice

350 g (12 oz) cod fillet, skinned and cut into 2.5 cm (1-inch) pieces
225 g (8 oz) salmon fillets, skinned and cut into 2.5 cm (1-inch) pieces
50 g ($1\frac{3}{4}$ oz) fresh white breadcrumbs
50 g ($1\frac{3}{4}$ oz) half-fat Cheddar or red Leicester cheese, grated
salt and freshly ground black pepper

1 Preheat the oven to Gas Mark 5/ 190°C/375°F.
2 Stir-fry the onion, celery and red pepper in the hot oil over a medium heat for 4–5 minutes, until softened but not browned.
3 Add all but a few tablespoons of the milk to the saucepan. Blend the remainder with the cornflour to give a smooth paste. Add this to the pan, stirring continuously over a moderate heat, until the milk comes to the boil and thickens. Remove from the heat and stir in the parsley and lemon or lime juice. Season to taste.

4 Arrange the fish in a 1.2 litre (2 pint) ovenproof dish and pour the sauce over. Mix together the breadcrumbs and cheese and scatter over the top. Cook for 30 minutes, until bubbling and the topping is golden brown and crispy. Serve immediately.

TOP TIP Divide the fish mixture and topping between four individual ovenproof dishes and freeze to enable you to defrost and use one or two servings at a time.

VARIATION For a Turkey and Mushroom Pie, replace the fish with 225 g (8 oz) button mushrooms and 450 g (1 lb) turkey pieces. Stir-fry with the vegetables at step 2. Add 1 teaspoon of Dijon mustard to the white sauce. This variation has $4\frac{1}{2}$ Points per serving.

WINTER SEAFOOD STEW

POINTS

per recipe: 14   per serving: $3\frac{1}{2}$

Serves 4
Preparation and cooking time: 25 minutes
Calories per serving: 235
Freezing: not recommended

This is a delicious 'stew' – good enough to serve on special occasions. As with all fish recipes, your choice of fish can be flexible to suit availability and preference! I like to use salmon, prawns and cod – and sometimes fresh mussels too, which are in season over the winter months. Serve with fluffy mashed potato (1 Point per scoop) and broccoli.

1 tablespoon olive oil
2 shallots or 1 medium onion, finely chopped
425 ml ($\frac{3}{4}$ pint) good quality fish or vegetable stock
4 tablespoons white wine
a large pinch of saffron strands (optional)
grated zest of $\frac{1}{2}$ lemon
225 g (8 oz) salmon fillets, skinned and cut into 4 cm ($1\frac{1}{2}$-inch) chunks
225 g (8 oz) cod or haddock fillets, skinned and cut into 4 cm ($1\frac{1}{2}$-inch) chunks
2 tablespoons half-fat crème fraîche
100 g ($3\frac{1}{2}$ oz) cooked peeled prawns
salt and freshly ground black pepper
1 tablespoon chopped fresh parsley or dill, to garnish

1 Heat the oil and gently cook the shallots or onion for 4–5 minutes until softened but not coloured. Add the stock, wine, saffron, if using, and lemon zest. Season lightly with salt and pepper. Bring to a gentle simmering point, and add the salmon and cod. Cover and poach for 2–3 minutes, or until the fish becomes opaque. Carefully remove the fish and keep warm.
2 Boil the stock rapidly, to reduce it to approximately 300 ml ($\frac{1}{2}$ pint). Stir in the crème fraîche and return the fish, together with the prawns, to the sauce. Heat through for 3–4 minutes. Adjust the seasoning to taste and serve, garnished with the parsley or dill.

As much as we love the carefree summer months of barbecues and salads, there is something comforting and cosy about drawing the curtains on dark nights, and looking forward to the ladling of steaming hot casseroles and hotpots into large bowls. There is no need to simmer or stew at the thought of long and laborious recipes – this chapter includes some quick mid-week favourites. All the recipes make the best of lean, low Point cuts of meat without compromising on flavour. Many of the recipes can be frozen until required. Remember, the flavour of stews and casseroles benefits from being eaten a day or two after cooking.

SAUSAGE AND LENTIL CASSEROLE

POINTS

per recipe: 19 per serving: $4\frac{1}{2}$

 if using vegetarian sausages
Serves 4
Preparation time: 15 minutes
Cooking time: 30 minutes
Calories per serving: 325
Freezing: recommended

How about preparing this recipe for Guy Fawkes night? It can be made well in advance, leaving you time to concentrate on other noisier bangers on the night…

Serve with a generous spoonful of mashed swede, which will not add any extra Points.

450 g pack 95% fat-free pork sausages
1 large onion, chopped
1 garlic clove, crushed
1 large carrot, coarsely grated
175 g (6 oz) Puy lentils
fresh thyme, to taste
400 g can chopped tomatoes
600 ml (1 pint) hot beef stock
4 tablespoons half-fat crème fraîche
salt and freshly ground black pepper

1 Prick the sausages all over, then dry-fry in a non-stick saucepan, until lightly coloured. Add the onion to the pan and continue to stir-fry until the onion is softened and golden. Add the garlic and carrot and cook for a further minute.
2 Stir in the lentils, thyme sprigs, chopped tomatoes and stock. Bring to the boil, then reduce the heat to a gentle simmer and cook, uncovered, for 30 minutes. Stir occasionally, adding a drop of water if the mixture becomes too dry. Season to taste.
3 When the casserole is ready to serve, stir in the crème fraîche.

TOP TIP Try Puy lentils, which you will find in good supermarkets. They require no soaking and taste great! Otherwise, green lentils or continental lentils are a good substitute.

VARIATION For a vegetarian option, use 2 × 250 g packs of Quorn sausages and vegetatable stock. Replace the beef stock with a good quality vegetable stock. The Points per serving will be $5\frac{1}{2}$.

Sausage and Lentil Casserole: This is sure to become a favourite at only 4½ Points per serving!

Meatball Goulash with Pasta: This easy dish is ideal for cosy nights in.

MEATBALL GOULASH WITH PASTA

POINTS

per recipe: **28**   per serving: **7**

Serves 4

Preparation time: 15 minutes

Cooking time: 35 minutes

Calories per serving: 425

Freezing: recommended (goulash only)

Make the most of lean low-fat pork and pile high these meatballs on to a bed of freshly cooked white cabbage and pasta. Finish with a ladle of the warming sauce.

FOR THE MEATBALLS

450 g (1 lb) lean minced pork

50 g (1¾ oz) fresh white breadcrumbs

1 small onion, grated

2 teaspoons paprika

1 garlic clove, chopped

1 medium egg, beaten

low-fat cooking spray

salt

FOR THE SAUCE

400 g can chopped tomatoes

1 tablespoon tomato purée

300 ml (½ pint) hot chicken or vegetable stock

1 teaspoon sugar

1 teaspoon chopped fresh sage (or ½ teaspoon dried)

salt

FOR THE PASTA MIXTURE

½ white cabbage or Savoy cabbage, finely shredded

200 g (7 oz) tagliatelle or spaghetti

1 Place all the meatball ingredients in a bowl and mix thoroughly. Roll small amounts in your hand to make 20 meatballs.

2 Heat a large non-stick frying-pan and spray with low-fat cooking spray. Fry the meatballs in batches to brown on all sides. Remove and drain on kitchen paper

3 To make the sauce, add the sauce ingredients to the frying-pan and bring to the boil. Simmer for 20 minutes. (Cover the pan if the sauce evaporates too quickly, but allow it to reduce and thicken slightly.)

4 Add the meatballs to the sauce and simmer for 10 minutes, stirring occasionally. Adjust the seasoning.

5 Meanwhile cook the cabbage in lightly salted water until just tender. Drain and refresh under cold running water. Cook the pasta in plenty of salted boiling water. Drain and return to the pan with the cabbage. Cover to keep warm in the steam.

6 Serve five meatballs covered in sauce with each serving and on a bed of the cabbage and pasta.

TOP TIP When you have odd ends of bread loaves, make them into breadcrumbs and store in the freezer in a rigid container. Simply measure out the required quantity.

VARIATION For a special occasion, or when you have saved sufficient Points that day, pour a tablespoon of half-fat crème fraîche over each portion of meatballs. Add ½ Point per serving.

IRISH STEW

POINTS

per recipe: $31^{1}/_{2}$ per serving: $5^{1}/_{2}$

Serves 6
Preparation time: 20 minutes
Cooking time: 1½ hours
Calories per serving: 425
Freezing: recommended

Only a short shopping list is required for this recipe! Choose the freshest ingredients to produce a simply delicious and filling stew.

low-fat cooking oil

6 × 175 g (6 oz) lean lamb chops, trimmed

1 tablespoon seasoned flour

4 large carrots, cut into large chunks

4 medium onions, quartered

4 sticks celery, cut into 2 cm (¾-inch) lengths

few sprigs of fresh thyme (or 2 teaspoons dried)

600 ml (1 pint) hot lamb stock

500 g (1 lb 2 oz) medium potatoes, quartered

2 teaspoons cornflour

1 tablespoon each of chopped fresh parsley and chives

salt and freshly ground black pepper

1 Preheat the oven to Gas Mark 4/ 180°C/350°F.

2 Spray a flameproof casserole dish with low-fat cooking spray and heat over moderate heat. Coat the chops with seasoned flour then seal both sides, two or three at a time if necessary. Layer all the lamb back in the casserole with the carrots, onions, celery and seasoning to taste. Tuck the sprigs of thyme in amongst the layers.

3 Pour the hot stock over, then arrange the potatoes on top of the casserole so that they steam while

the stew cooks. Bring to the boil on top of the hob then transfer to the oven and cook for 1¼–1½ hours, or until the meat and vegetables are tender.

4 Carefully pour the cooking liquid into a small saucepan skimming away any grease, and bring to the boil. Stir in the cornflour and cook for a minute, until the stock thickens slightly. Adjust the seasoning, stir in the parsley and chives and pour over the stew. Serve immediately.

TOP TIP You can now purchase fresh chilled lamb stock from most supermarkets. All fresh stocks freeze well, and are a handy stand-by at this time of year.

Irish Stew: A traditional favourite for only 5½ Points per serving.

BRAISED PORK CASEROLE

POINTS

per recipe: 18½   per serving: 4½

Serves 4
Preparation time: 10 minutes
Cooking time: 50 minutes
Calories per serving (with crème fraîche): 275
Freezing: recommended

An ideal recipe for the winter months. This is delicious and indulgent enough to serve on special occasions without your guests knowing it is low in Points.

1 tablespoon vegetable oil
1 large onion, chopped
500 g (1 lb 2 oz) lean pork, cut into 2.5 cm (1-inch) cubes
4 sticks celery, cut into 2 cm (¾-inch) slices
1 large sprig fresh sage or rosemary
1 medium Bramley apple, peeled and sliced thickly
1 eating apple i.e. Cox's, peeled and sliced thickly
300 ml (½ pint) dry cider or unsweetened apple juice
2 teaspoons cornflour
2 tablespoons half-fat crème fraîche (optional)
salt and freshly ground black pepper
1 tablespoon chopped fresh sage or rosemary, to garnish

1 Preheat the oven to Gas Mark 5/ 190°C/375°F. Heat the oil in a flameproof casserole. Add the onion and pork and stir-fry until the meat has coloured and the onion softened.

2 Add the celery and fresh herb sprig, and toss over the heat for 2–3 minutes. Stir in the apples and cider or apple juice. Season to taste with salt and pepper.

3 Cover tightly and cook in the oven for 50 minutes or until the meat is tender and the apples are beginning to break up.

4 Remove the herb sprig. Blend the cornflour with a drop of water and stir this into the casserole. Transfer the casserole to a moderate heat on the hob and heat until the sauce thickens slightly. Adjust the seasoning to taste.

5 Just before serving, swirl in the crème fraîche, if using, and garnish with the chopped fresh herbs.

TOP TIP Bramley apples cook down to a pulp very quickly so add an eating apple, which holds its shape well, to get a chunkier texture. This works well for both apple sauce and pie fillings.

VARIATIONS For those of you who like celeriac, replace the celery with 225 g (8 oz) of this delicious vegetable, peeled and cut into 2 cm (¾-inch) chunks.

By omitting the crème fraîche you will reduce your Points per serving to 4.

CHINESE-STYLE LAMB

POINTS

per recipe: 22   per serving: 5½

Serves 4
Preparation time: 10 minutes
Cooking time: 35–40 minutes
Calories per serving: 260
Freezing: recommended

East meets West in this tasty dish with lamb. Mop up the juices with plain boiled rice (4 tablespoons is 3 Points) and boiled Chinese leaf or pak choi, adding the extra Points per serving.

450 g (1 lb) lean lamb neck fillet, cut into chunks

FOR THE COOKING LIQUID

5 cm (2-inch) strip of lemon or orange rind
50 ml (2 fl oz) soy sauce
2 tablespoons dry sherry
2 teaspoons soft brown sugar
2 spring onions, cut into 5 cm (2-inch) pieces
2.5 cm (1-inch) piece of fresh root ginger, chopped
1 level teaspoon ground cinnamon
1 tablespoon fresh chopped chives, to garnish

1 Put all the ingredients for the cooking liquid in a flameproof casserole dish or saucepan, add 125 ml (4 fl oz) of water and bring to the boil. Add the lamb, cover, reduce the heat to a gentle simmer and cook for 35–40 minutes or until the meat is tender.

2 Remove the lamb to four individual plates to keep warm. Boil the cooking juices rapidly until reduced by half. Strain over the lamb and serve, garnished with some chopped chives.

TOP TIP Fresh root ginger has a wonderful flavour, and will keep well in the fridge salad drawer for frequent use (great in stir-fries and salad dressings). However, I like to thinly slice or grate the ginger and store it in a re-sealable bag in the freezer.

VARIATION The cooking liquid is really versatile to use with duck, chicken or pork. Remember to adjust the Points accordingly.

BEEF IN BEER WITH DUMPLINGS

POINTS

| per recipe: $25\frac{1}{2}$ | per serving: $6\frac{1}{2}$ |

Serves 4
Preparation time: 25 minutes
Cooking time: 2 hours
Calories per serving: 405
Freezing: recommended

To think that beef stew and dumplings was once regarded as an economical, filling meal for all the family! Now you will find variations in top restaurants and food magazines – how trends have changed. Serve with Point-free carrots and cabbage for a great traditional meal.

1 tablespoon vegetable oil
500 g (1 lb 2 oz) lean braising steak, cubed
2 medium onions, cut into chunks
2 celery sticks, chopped
1 tablespoon plain flour
300 ml (½ pint) strong dark ale
300 ml (½ pint) beef stock
1 bay leaf
a few sprigs fresh thyme or 1 teaspoon dried thyme
250 g (9 oz) open mushrooms, halved
salt and freshly ground black pepper

FOR THE DUMPLINGS

100 g (3½ oz) plain flour
a pinch of salt
2 teaspoons dried mustard powder
40 g (1½ oz) low-fat spread (e.g. St Ivel 'Gold')
1 tablespoon finely chopped fresh chives

1 Preheat the oven to Gas Mark 3/ 170°C/325°F. Heat the oil in a flameproof casserole dish and brown the meat all over. Remove with a slotted spoon. Add the onions and celery and cook for 5 minutes, stirring occasionally.

2 Sprinkle in the flour, and gradually blend in the beer and stock. Add the bay leaf and thyme. Season with salt and pepper. Cover and transfer to the oven to cook for 1½ hours.

3 Meanwhile, make the dumplings. Sift the flour, salt and mustard into a bowl. Rub in the low-fat spread until the mixture resembles fine breadcrumbs. Stir in the chives and add just enough cold water to make a soft dough. Shape into eight small dumplings. Chill until required.

4 After 1½ hours, remove the lid from the casserole, stir in the mushrooms and adjust the seasoning, to taste. Increase the oven temperature to Gas Mark 6/200°C/400°F. Arrange the dumplings over the surface of

the casserole and transfer to the highest shelf of the oven, without the lid and cook for a further 30 minutes until the dumplings are golden brown and crusty.

TOP TIP If you have a slow cooker, this recipe lends itself to long gentle cooking, so adapt the recipe according to the manufacturer's instructions.

VARIATION Vary the dumplings by replacing the mustard and chives with the same quantity of horseradish and parsley.

Beef in Beer with Dumplings: Comfort food at its best and only 6½ Points per serving.

SWEET AND SPICY PORK

POINTS

per recipe: 21½   per serving: 5½

Serves 4
Preparation time: 20 minutes
Cooking time: 30 minutes
Calories per serving: 375
Freezing: recommended

Pile this fragrant, sweet casserole on to a bed of steaming couscous, and enjoy the sultry heat of the Middle East.

1 teaspoon olive oil
1 large onion, halved and sliced
2 tablespoons seasoned flour
1 teaspoon ground ginger
450 g (1 lb) pork fillet, sliced into 2 cm (³⁄₄-inch) rounds
1 garlic clove, crushed
2 teaspoons harissa paste
425 ml (³⁄₄ pint) hot vegetable or chicken stock
1 tablespoon tomato purée
6 ready-to-eat apricots, halved
2 tablespoons chopped fresh coriander or sage leaves
salt

FOR THE COUSCOUS

175 g (6 oz) couscous
4 saffron strands (optional)
300 ml (½ pint) hot vegetable stock
2 tablespoons snipped fresh chives
salt and freshly ground black pepper

1 Heat the oil in a heavy-based saucepan or flameproof casserole. Cook the onion for 5 minutes, until softened and slightly golden.

2 Meanwhile, put the seasoned flour and the ginger in a plastic bag with the pork. Shake well to coat and remove the meat, shaking off any excess flour. Add the meat to the pan with the garlic and stir-fry over a high heat for 3–4 minutes, until the pork has browned.

3 Add the harissa paste and cook for a further minute before stirring in the stock and the tomato purée. Bring to the boil, then reduce the heat, cover and simmer gently for 15 minutes. Add the apricots, coriander or sage, season to taste, and simmer for a further 10 minutes.

4 Meanwhile, place the couscous in a heatproof bowl with the saffron, if using. Pour the hot stock over and leave for 5 minutes to soak. Stir in the chives with a fork (this will also fluff up the grains) and season to taste.

5 Spoon the couscous into warmed bowls and pile on the pork. Serve at once.

TOP TIP Harissa paste is made up of a lively combination of Middle Eastern spices. It adds a great flavour – and heat too! Keep a tube or jar handy for instant authenticity.

VARIATION If you want a change from 'heat' and 'spice', replace the harissa with 2 tablespoons dark soy sauce and a dash of Tabasco sauce.

ROAST HAM WITH SPICY PLUM GLAZE

POINTS

per recipe: 36½   per serving: 4½

Serves 8
Preparation time: 10 minutes
Cooking time: 3 hours
Calories per serving: 350
Freezing: recommended

Leftover ham can be used for tasty sandwich fillings, or tossed into a mid-week pasta bake. A great Christmas centrepiece too!

2.25 kg (5 lb) unsmoked gammon joint

FOR THE GLAZE

125 g (4½ oz) plum jam
2 tablespoons orange, lemon or apple juice
1 teaspoon ground ginger
2 teaspoons chilli sauce

1 Preheat the oven to Gas Mark 5/ 180°C/375°F.

2 Wrap the gammon joint in foil and place in a roasting tin. Roast in the oven for 3 hours (65 minutes per kilo/30 minutes per lb, plus 30 minutes extra).

3 To make the glaze, place all the ingredients in a small pan and gently heat together.

4 Remove the foil for the last 30 minutes of cooking, brush half the glaze over the joint and return to the oven, uncovered. Repeat 10 minutes later.

5 At the end of the cooking time, remove the ham to a serving platter, and brush any remaining glaze from the roasting pan over the top. Carve into thin slices, and serve 175 g (6 oz) ham per person.

TOP TIP For a cold-eating joint, cook the ham up to three days in advance, wrap in foil and refrigerate until required. It is also much easier to carve when completely cold!

VARIATION For an alternative glaze, replace the plum jam with orange marmalade, omit the chilli sauce and add a teaspoon of allspice or ground cinnamon with the ginger.

POTATO-TOPPED CHILLI BEEF

POINTS

per recipe: 24	per serving: 6

Serves 4
Preparation time: 10 minutes
Cooking time: 1 hour 50 minutes
Calories per serving: 390
Freezing: recommended (after step 2)

Delicious accompanied by fresh vegetables or a crisp green salad.

450 g (1 lb) lean braising beef, cut into cubes

1 large onion, cut into chunks

2 garlic cloves, crushed

400 g can chopped tomatoes

400 g can red kidney beans, drained

300 ml (½ pint) hot beef stock

2 teaspoons hot chilli powder

2 whole green chillies

2 medium red peppers, de-seeded and cut into chunks

2 teaspoons cornflour, blended to a paste with a little cold water

salt and freshly ground black pepper

FOR THE TOPPING

280 g pack frozen jacket potato wedges

50 g (1¾ oz) half-fat Cheddar cheese

1 Preheat the oven to Gas Mark 4/ 180°C/350°F.

2 Place all the ingredients except the red peppers, cornflour paste and topping ingredients in a large ovenproof casserole. Mix well, cover and cook in the oven for 1½ hours, or until the meat is tender.

3 Remove the whole chillies, season to taste, then stir in the red peppers and cornflour paste. Place the potato wedges on top and sprinkle with the cheese. Return to the oven and cook, uncovered, for a further 20 minutes or until the wedges are crispy and the cheese has melted, then serve.

VARIATION Accompany with a 150 g carton of low-fat plain yogurt mixed with chopped fresh chives or coriander and the zest of ½ lime. Add ½ Point per serving.

ROASTED LAMB STEAKS

POINTS

per recipe: 10	per serving: 5

Serves 2
Preparation time: 10 minutes
Cooking time: 45 minutes
Calories per serving: 470
Freezing: not recommended

Serve with broccoli or cabbage.

1 medium potato, cut into 8 wedges

1 medium parsnip, quartered lengthways

1 large carrot, quartered lengthways

1 medium red onion, quartered

2 sticks celery, cut into 5 cm (2-inch) lengths

2 garlic cloves

low-fat cooking spray

sprigs of fresh rosemary and thyme

2 × 150 g (5½ oz) lean lamb steaks

salt and freshly ground black pepper

FOR THE GLAZE

1 tablespoon redcurrant jelly or mint jelly

juice of 1 orange

1 Preheat the oven to Gas Mark 6/ 200°C/400°F.

2 Blanch the potato, parsnip, carrot and onion in boiling, lightly salted water for 5 minutes. Drain (reserving the cooking water if serving with gravy), and refresh in cold water. Drain again, thoroughly.

3 Place all the vegetables including the garlic in a shallow roasting tray. Spray with the low-fat cooking spray. Roast for 15 minutes.

4 Meanwhile, melt the redcurrant or mint jelly in a small pan and stir in the orange juice. Remove the vegetables from the oven and brush with the glaze. Season well with plenty of black pepper.

5 Tuck the sprigs of fresh herbs amongst the vegetables and lay the lamb steaks on top, brushing them with a little glaze. Return the tray to the oven to roast for a further 15 minutes. Turn the steaks over, brush any remaining glaze on top and return to the oven for a final 15 minutes.

6 Serve the lamb steaks on a bed of the roasted vegetables.

Potato-topped Chilli Beef: A dish worth staying in for!

TOP TIP By blanching the root vegetables, you will reduce the roasting time by 15–20 minutes.

VARIATION Replace the lamb with two part-boned skinless chicken breasts, each approximately 200 g (7 oz). This will give 4½ Points per serving.

Aubergine,
Tomato and
Mozzarella
Bake: Only 1½
Points per
serving!

vital veggies

I love my meat-free meals – enjoying the flavour of fresh vegetables with other tasty ingredients I would not usually eat much of – like cheese, a savoury crumble topping or chick-peas. Sometimes it can be hard to think of meat-free recipes which are both nutritious and satisfying but hopefully this chapter will help you to realise that there are delicious, easy and warming alternatives to meat and poultry. You will find particular reference is made to the abundance of seasonal vegetables which we are fortunate enough to enjoy during the winter months.

Why not freeze individual portions to treat yourself on the nights in on your own? Try the recommended variations and extend your repertoire to help see you through to the spring months!

AUBERGINE, TOMATO AND MOZZARELLA BAKE

POINTS	
per recipe: 10	per serving: $1^{1}/_{2}$

Ⓥ *Serves 6*
Preparation time: 15 minutes
Cooking time: 1½ hours including sauce
Calories per serving: 160

Enjoy a touch of Italian sunshine on a winter evening; this is an ideal supper to enjoy with friends – or on a tray in front of the TV. Serve with a crisp green salad to keep the Points low.

2 × 400 g cans chopped tomatoes
2 garlic cloves, crushed
2 tablespoons chopped fresh basil (or 1 teaspoon dried)
1 teaspoon grated lemon rind
a pinch of sugar
4 large red peppers, de-seeded and quartered
1 tablespoon olive oil
3 aubergines, sliced into 2 cm (¾-inch) rounds
125 g (4½ oz) mozzarella 'light' cheese, drained and thinly sliced
50 g (2 oz) freshly grated parmesan cheese
salt and freshly ground black pepper

1 Place the tomatoes in a saucepan with the garlic, basil, lemon rind and sugar. Season well. Cover and simmer for 30 minutes then remove the lid and simmer for a further 15 minutes. Cool.

2 Preheat the oven to Gas Mark 6/ 200°C/400°F.

3 Place the peppers, skin side up, on a grill pan, brush lightly with oil and grill for 4–5 minutes until charred and blistered. Transfer to a bowl, cover with clingfilm and leave to cool. Brush the aubergine slices with the remaining oil and grill for 5–6 minutes on each side then remove from the heat and leave to cool. Peel the peppers.

4 Spoon a little tomato sauce into the base of a large, shallow ovenproof dish and top with a layer of peppers and aubergine. Arrange half the mozzarella slices over then repeat, with more vegetables, finishing with the mozzarella. Sprinkle with parmesan.

5 Bake in the oven for 30–40 minutes, until bubbling and golden brown. Serve immediately.

CHEESE, ONION AND TOMATO BREAD PUDDING

POINTS

per recipe: 45½   per serving: 7½

Ⓥ *if using vegetarian cheese and free-range eggs*

Serves 6
Preparation time: 10 minutes
Cooking time: 45 minutes
Calories per serving: 445
Freezing: not recommended

A great family stand-by.

low-fat cooking spray
300 g (10½ oz) French bread, sliced
700 ml (1¼ pints) skimmed milk
2 × 400 g cans chopped tomatoes
2 teaspoons dried Italian herbs or herbes de Provence
1 large garlic clove, crushed
350 g (12 oz) half-fat Cheddar cheese, grated
6 medium eggs, beaten
salt and freshly ground black pepper

1 Preheat the oven to Gas Mark 4/ 180°C/350°F. Spray a shallow ovenproof baking dish (approximately 30 × 25 cm/ 12 × 10-inches) with the low-fat cooking spray.

2 Cut the bread into 5 mm (¼-inch) diagonal slices. Pour half the milk into a shallow dish.

3 Mix the tomatoes, herbs, garlic and plenty of seasoning together in a bowl. Dip each bread slice in the milk and use half to arrange in a single layer to cover the base of the dish. Spoon about half of the tomato mixture over the bread, and cover with a layer of cheese. Repeat the three layers once more, finishing with the cheese.

4 Add any remaining milk to the eggs. Season and pour over the bread mixture. Cook for 45 minutes, or until the bread is puffed up, bubbling and golden brown. Remove from the oven and allow to rest for 5 minutes before serving.

TOP TIP Day-old French bread is best for this recipe – its light texture is ideal.

Tomato and Basil Risotto: A warming and delicious Italian speciality.

TOMATO AND BASIL RISOTTO

POINTS

per recipe: 6½   per serving: 3

Serves 2
Preparation time: 10 minutes
Cooking time: 25 minutes
Calories per serving: 260
Freezing: not recommended

Here is a foolproof recipe for a fresh, easy dish to enjoy for lunch or supper. Serve with a crisp green salad or some freshly cooked spinach.

low-fat cooking spray
40 g (1½ oz) onion, chopped finely
1 garlic clove, crushed
100 g (3½ oz) Arborio rice or risotto rice
300 ml (½ pint) tomato juice
200 ml (7 fl oz) vegetable stock
1 tablespoon sun-dried tomato purée
2 ripe tomatoes, peeled, de-seeded and diced
2 tablespoons virtually-fat-free fromage frais
2 tablespoons fresh, torn basil leaves plus 4 whole leaves, to garnish
salt and freshly ground black pepper

1 Spray the low-fat cooking spray in a non-stick saucepan. Add the onion and garlic and cook gently for 5 minutes or until softened but not coloured. Add the rice, and cook for a further minute stirring frequently. The rice will become opaque.

2 In a small saucepan, heat the tomato juice and stock to simmering point. Add a ladle of the liquid to the rice and stir continuously until all the liquid has been used. Repeat, stirring after each addition, until all the liquid has been absorbed. The rice will become tender and creamy.

3 Stir in the tomato purée, fresh tomatoes, fromage frais and basil. Season well. Serve immediately garnished with the basil leaves.

TOP TIP Arborio rice is the classic short, stubby grain used to give risotto its characteristic creamy texture. Italian-style easy-cook rice also gives good results

VARIATION Add 50 g (1¾ oz) chopped mushrooms together with the last addition of tomato juice. Use 1 tablespoon of freshly grated parmesan to sprinkle over the risotto. This will increase your Points per serving to 4½.

Cheese, Onion
and Tomato
Bread Pudding:
A good old-
fashioned
pudding with
a fantastic
savoury twist!

Root Vegetable Bake: Serve with a mustard sauce and fresh green vegetables for a great supper.

ROOT VEGETABLE BAKE

POINTS

per recipe: 12	per serving: 3

Ⓥ if not using the creamy mustard sauce

Serves 4 as a main meal
Preparation time: 40 minutes
Cooking time: 50 minutes
Calories per serving: 515
Freezing: recommended for the bake only

Delicious too, as an accompaniment to grilled and roast meats for six and the Points per serving will be 2.

225 g (8 oz) potatoes
225 g (8 oz) celeriac (optional)
1 medium swede
2 large carrots
2 medium parsnips
2 large onions
4 small turnips
low-fat cooking spray
2 teaspoons chopped fresh thyme or rosemary (or 1 teaspoon dried)
200 ml (7 fl oz) hot vegetable stock
200 ml (7 fl oz) semi-skimmed milk
25 g (1 oz) low-fat spread
salt and freshly ground black pepper

FOR THE CREAMY MUSTARD SAUCE (OPTIONAL)

25 g (1 oz) low-fat spread
25 g (1 oz) plain or sauce flour
300 ml (½ pint) skimmed milk
2 teaspoons wholegrain mustard
1 teaspoon Dijon mustard
2 tablespoons virtually-fat-free fromage frais
salt and white pepper

1 Preheat the oven to Gas Mark 4/ 180°C/350°F.

2 Peel and cut all the vegetables into wafer-thin slices. Cook in a large pan of lightly salted boiling water for 5 minutes, then drain thoroughly. Spray a large lasagne dish or a roasting dish with low-fat cooking spray. Arrange the assorted vegetables in layers with the thyme and plenty of seasoning.

3 Pour in the stock and milk. Fleck the surface all over with the low-fat spread.

4 Transfer to the highest shelf in the oven and cook for 45–50 minutes, or until the vegetables are very tender and the surface is brown and crispy.

5 Meanwhile, if using, make the sauce. Place the low-fat spread, the flour and the milk in a small pan and bring to simmering point, stirring all the time. Bring to the boil, still stirring, until the sauce thickens. Stir in the mustards, fromage frais and seasoning to taste. Do not allow the sauce to boil.

6 Serve slices of the bake accompanied with the Creamy Mustard Sauce if using

VARIATION With the exception of potatoes, use whatever combination and quantity of vegetables you prefer. Replace the celeriac with the same weight in celery and additional carrot. The Points will remain the same.

MUSHROOM AND LEEK CRUMBLE

POINTS

per recipe: 8½   per serving: 4

V *if using vegetarian cheese*
Serves 2
Preparation time: 15 minutes
Cooking time: 30 minutes
Calories per serving: 325
Freezing: not recommended

Here's another TV supper to enjoy. Mushrooms and leeks topped with a golden crumble topping. Serve with fresh vegetables or a green salad.

low-fat cooking spray
6 open, field mushrooms, halved and sliced thickly
2 medium leeks, sliced thickly
1 garlic clove, crushed
400 g can chopped tomatoes with herbs
1 tablespoon tomato purée
½ teaspoon dried mixed herbs
salt and freshly ground black pepper

FOR THE CRUMBLE
50 g (1¾ oz) plain flour
25 g (1 oz) rolled oats
½ teaspoon mustard powder
15 g (½ oz) low-fat spread (e.g. St Ivel 'Gold')
50 g (1¾ oz) half-fat Cheddar cheese

1 Preheat the oven to Gas Mark 5/ 190°C/375°F. Spray a saucepan with the low-fat cooking spray, add the mushroom and leeks and stir-fry for 5 minutes, or until softened. Add the garlic and cook for a further minute or two.

2 Stir in the tomatoes, purée and herbs. Season with salt and pepper. Cover and simmer for 10 minutes.

3 To make the crumble place the flour, oats, mustard powder and low-fat spread in a bowl and rub together until the mixture becomes crumbly. Mix in the cheese. Season with a little salt and pepper.

4 Pour the tomato mixture into a 600 ml (1-pint) shallow ovenproof dish. Cover with the crumble. Cook the crumble for 30 minutes or until the topping is golden and crisp.

BAKED FETA AND TOMATO MARROW

POINTS

per recipe: 14½   per serving: 3½

Serves 4
Preparation time: 15 minutes
Cooking time: 30 minutes
Calories per serving: 230
Freezing: recommended for the tomato sauce only

Try this delicious recipe – served with a robust tomato and herb sauce – accompanied by fresh green beans.

FOR THE TOMATO SAUCE
400 g can chopped tomatoes
1 small onion, finely chopped
1 stick celery, finely chopped
1 small carrot, finely chopped
½ garlic clove, chopped
a small bunch of fresh parsley
a dash of Worcestershire sauce
1 teaspoon caster sugar
2 teaspoons chopped fresh thyme (or ½ teaspoon dried)
salt and freshly ground black pepper

FOR THE MARROW
675 g (1½ lb) marrow, peeled, de-seeded and cut into 5 cm (1-inch) rings
1 medium onion, finely chopped
1 tablespoon vegetable oil
1 garlic clove, chopped
175 g (6 oz) mushrooms, roughly chopped
175 g (6 oz) cooked long-grain rice
1 teaspoon chopped fresh rosemary (or ½ teaspoon dried)
100 g (3½ oz) feta cheese, crumbled

1 Put all the ingredients for the tomato sauce in a heavy-based saucepan, cover and simmer over a gentle heat for 30 minutes. Liquidise the sauce and return to the pan. Adjust the seasoning to taste. If it is too thin, reduce by boiling rapidly. Keep warm.

2 Meanwhile preheat the oven to Gas Mark 6/200°C/400°F. Cook the marrow in boiling salted water for 3–4 minutes, or until tender. Drain thoroughly, drying on kitchen towel then arrange in a shallow ovenproof dish.

3 Cook the onion in the oil in a frying-pan until soft. Add the garlic and cook for a further minute before stirring in the mushrooms. Increase the heat and stir-fry the mushrooms, evaporating off any liquid released from the mushrooms.

4 Stir in the rice and rosemary. Divide between the marrow rings and sprinkle over the feta cheese. Bake in the oven for 12–15 minutes, or until piping hot and golden brown.

5 Serve immediately with the tomato sauce.

VARIATION Replace the feta cheese with 175 g (6 oz) cooked, peeled prawns, chopped and added with the rice. This will reduce the Points per serving to 2½.

FESTIVE VEGETABLE BOURGUIGNON

POINTS	
per recipe: 16	per serving: 4

Ⓥ Serves 4

Preparation time: 15 minutes

Cooking time: 35–40 minutes

Calories per serving: 300

Freezing: not recommended

This is a special dish – perfect for Christmas and rich in flavours and colour. Ladle into bowls and serve with fresh green vegetables or a Brussels sprout purée.

225 g (8oz) sweet potato, cut into 5 cm (2-inch) chunks

225 g (8oz) parsnips, cut into 5 cm (2-inch) chunks

225 g (8oz) large button mushrooms, left whole

225 g (8oz) small carrots, halved lengthways

8 shallots, peeled

2 small leeks, cut into 5 cm (2-inch) lengths

125 g (4½ oz) ready-to-eat prunes

125 g (4½ oz) canned peeled chestnuts

25 g (1 oz) seasoned flour

1 tablespoon olive oil

400 ml (14 fl oz) hot vegetable stock

200 ml (7 fl oz) red wine

1 bouquet garni

salt and freshly ground black pepper

fresh chopped parsley, to garnish

1 Preheat the oven to Gas Mark 3/ 170°C/325°F.

2 Place all the vegetables, prunes and chestnuts in a large shallow dish and sprinkle on the flour. Toss them to give them an even coating.

3 Heat the oil in a large flameproof casserole. Brown the vegetables, prunes and chestnuts a few at a time. Return the mixture to the casserole dish and pour over the stock and wine. Tuck in the bouquet garni. Season to taste with salt and plenty of black pepper. Bring to the boil on the hob then transfer to the oven for 35 minutes or until the vegetables and chestnuts are tender.

4 Use a slotted spoon to divide the mixture between four shallow bowls. Remove the bouquet garni, and rapidly boil the juices to reduce them to a syrupy consistency. Check the seasoning and spoon over the vegetable mixture. Garnish with plenty of parsley and serve immediately.

TOP TIP Sweet potatoes originate in South America. Delicious and under-utilised, they are readily available in all good supermarkets. Remember you can grill them on the barbecue too, come the summer months!

VARIATIONS If you love the flavour of garlic, add 2 or 3 cloves after the vegetables have been browned, however the flavour will be quite dominant.

Substitute the prunes with apricots and the wine with cider for a lighter flavour.

SPINACH, EGG AND CHEESE RAMEKINS

POINTS	
per recipe: 12	per serving: 3

Ⓥ if using vegetarian cheese and free-range eggs

Serves 4

Preparation time and cooking time: 15 minutes

Calories per serving: 210

Freezing: not recommended

Balance the heartier winter dishes with this light savoury supper.

4 medium eggs

675 g (1½ lb) spinach

50 g (1¾ oz) mature Cheddar cheese, grated

salt and freshly ground black pepper

FOR THE SAUCE

400 g can chopped tomatoes

1 tablespoon finely chopped onion

½ teaspoon dried oregano or basil

½ teaspoon sugar

3 tablespoons virtually-fat-free fromage frais

1 To make the sauce place the tomatoes, onion, herbs and sugar in a small pan and bring to the boil, then simmer for 10 minutes. Season to taste with salt and pepper. Blend the sauce to a purée in a liquidiser or food processor. Beat in the fromage frais.

2 Meanwhile, place the eggs in a pan of boiling water and boil for 4 minutes. Shell and keep them in a bowl of warm water.

3 Cook the spinach in a small amount of boiling water for 3–4 minutes or until tender. Drain well and chop. Divide between four 10 cm (4-inch) ramekins, making a dip in the centre of each. Place an egg in each 'nest'.

4 Spoon the hot sauce over the eggs. Sprinkle on the cheese and place under a pre-heated grill for 3–4 minutes until the cheese has melted and is bubbling. Serve immediately.

WINTER VEGETABLE KORMA

POINTS

per recipe: 11	per serving: 2½

(V) Serves 4

Preparation time: 10 minutes

Cooking time: 20 minutes

Calories per serving: 240

Freezing: recommended after step 2

Korma is one of the mildest (and creamiest) of curries. Enjoy this 'warm' dish with either 4 tablespoons plain boiled rice (3 Points) or ½ medium naan bread for 4 Points.

1 tablespoon vegetable oil

2 large onions, sliced

2 garlic cloves, crushed

1 tablespoon ground cumin

1 tablespoon ground coriander

1 teaspoon ground turmeric

1 teaspoon ground ginger or a 4 cm (1½-inch) piece fresh ginger, grated

1 tablespoon plain flour

450 ml (¾ pint) vegetable stock

1 tablespoon tomato purée

225 g (8 oz) carrots, sliced

225 g (8 oz) parsnips, chopped

275 g (9½ oz) cauliflower florets

425 g can chick-peas, drained

110 g (4 oz) button mushrooms, halved

4 tablespoons low-fat plain yogurt

salt

2 tablespoons chopped fresh coriander or parsley, to garnish

1 Heat the oil in a large pan, add the onions and cook gently for 5 minutes, until softened and golden. Add the garlic and stir in the ground spices. Cook for a minute. Sprinkle on the flour and cook for a further minute

2 Blend in the vegetable stock until smooth, add the tomato purée, carrots and parsnips. Bring to the boil, cover and simmer for 10 minutes. Add the cauliflower, chick-peas and mushrooms and simmer for a further 10 minutes.

3 Season with salt, take the pan off the heat and lightly swirl in the yogurt.

Serve garnished with the chopped herbs.

TOP TIP For a hotter curry, add ½–1 teaspoon chilli powder at step 1 with the other spices. For a quick Korma, replace all the vegetables with frozen mixed vegetables, adding ½ Point per 100 g (3½ oz).

Winter Vegetable Korma: Increase the heat with extra spices if you wish; you can vary the vegetables for a change too.

HOT SPICED CHICK-PEAS

POINTS

per recipe: 6	per serving: 3

(V) Serves 2

Preparation time: 5 minutes

Cooking time: 15 minutes

Calories per serving: 205

Freezing: not recommended

This spicy meal is delicious served with 1 medium slice of bread (1 Point) and salad, or 4 tablespoons plain boiled rice (3 Points). Remember to add the extra Points per serving.

1 teaspoon olive oil

1 small onion, chopped

1 teaspoon turmeric

½ teaspoon cumin seeds

1 teaspoon garam masala

4 large firm tomatoes, chopped roughly

425 g can chick-peas, drained

2 teaspoons lemon juice

2 tablespoon chopped fresh coriander

salt and freshly ground black pepper

coriander leaves, to garnish

1 Heat the oil in a small saucepan, add the onion and cook for 5–10 minutes, stirring constantly, until golden brown.

2 Add the spices and cook for a further minute. Add the tomatoes, chick-peas, lemon juice and coriander. Season well, to taste. Cook for 1–2 minutes.

3 Spoon into a warmed bowl, garnish with coriander and serve immediately.

TOP TIP Buy spices in small quantities as both the colour and flavour deteriorate over time. Store them in a dark dry cupboard. Start with a good basic range and increase the selection as you begin to experiment with new flavours.

VARIATION For a light snack for four, divide the spicy chick-peas between four medium baked potatoes, and garnish each with 1 tablespoon of low-fat plain yogurt. This will be 4 Points per serving.

Browse through just some of these recipes and you will find that many of those traditional, indulgent and 'stodgy' puddings can now be enjoyed as part of *pure points*™.

STEAMED CHOCOLATE CASTLES

POINTS

per recipe: 31½   per serving: 5½

V *if using free-range eggs*
Serves 6
Preparation time: 10 minutes +
20 minutes standing time
Cooking time: 15–20 minutes
Calories per serving: 315
Freezing: not recommended

Invest in some small moulds or ramekin dishes to make these little puddings. They will become a huge success with the whole family. Crown the tops with the delicious vanilla sauce.

low-fat cooking spray

75 g (2¾ oz) dark chocolate (minimum 70% cocoa solids)

150 ml (¼ pint) skimmed milk

150 g (5½ oz) Madeira sponge cake, crumbled

50 g (1¾ oz) low-fat spread

50 g (1¾ oz) caster sugar

2 medium eggs, separated

2 drops vanilla essence

FOR THE SAUCE

2 level tablespoons sauce flour

1 tablespoon caster sugar

425 ml (¾ pint) skimmed milk

a few drops of vanilla essence

1 Lightly spray six moulds or 8 cm (3-inch) ramekin dishes with the low-fat cooking spray.

2 Place the chocolate into a saucepan with the milk and heat gently until melted. Stir, then bring to the boil. Pour the chocolate mixture over the cake crumbs and leave to stand for 20 minutes.

3 Put the low-fat spread and sugar into a small bowl and beat together until light and creamy. Beat in the egg yolks, vanilla essence and cake crumb mixture. Whisk the egg whites until stiff then carefully fold into the mixture.

4 Divide between the moulds or ramekin dishes, cover with a piece of greaseproof paper and place in a steamer (see 'Variation' if you do not have a steamer). Steam for 15–20 minutes or until lightly set.

5 To make the sauce, blend the flour and sugar with a little of the milk to a smooth paste in a small saucepan.

Whisk in the remaining milk and stir over a moderate heat until the sauce comes to a boil. Allow the sauce to boil for 1 minute, stirring all the time as it becomes thick and smooth. Remove from the heat then stir in the vanilla essence.

6 Turn the steamed puddings out on to individual plates and drizzle the sauce over the top.

TOP TIP Steaming is the healthiest method of cooking. Not only is it quick but also, when cooking vegetables and fruit, it preserves a high proportion of nutrients compared to other conventional methods. The flavours and textures of all steamed food are superb too. You will find that most steaming recipes are naturally low in fat, which has to be good!

VARIATIONS If you do not have a steamer, cover and cook the moulds in a preheated oven (Gas Mark 6/ 200°C/400°F) in a roasting tin filled with 2.5 cm (1-inch) of water for 15–20 minutes.

For a creamier sauce, stir in 2 tablespoons of half-fat crème fraîche. The Points per serving will be the same.

Steamed
Chocolate
Castles: Moist
and chocolately
heaven!

1 Place the rice and milk in a pan and bring to the boil, stirring constantly. Simmer gently for 30–40 minutes or until tender, adding a little extra milk if necessary. Stir in the sugar and vanilla essence.

2 Quarter the apricot halves and divide between the bases of four 125 ml (4 fl oz) ramekin dishes. Top with the rice pudding.

3 Mix together the orange rind, spice, sugar and almonds and sprinkle evenly over the rice pudding.

4 Transfer the ramekins to a baking sheet and place under a preheated hot grill for 5 minutes, or until the sugar has caramelised and is bubbling and golden. Serve while still warm – or chill.

TOP TIP Use the above basic recipe for rice pudding to serve with stewed fruits or a spoonful of sultanas or reduced-sugar jam. On its own, the rice pudding is 2 Points per serving.

VARIATIONS Use 250 g (9 oz) fresh raspberries instead of the apricots and omit the orange rind from the topping. Points per serving will be the same.

For a special occasion, stir in 4 tablespoons half-fat crème fraîche. Points per serving will be 4.

Apricot and Almond Rice Pudding Crunch: A lovely twist on the nostalgic rice pudding.

APRICOT AND ALMOND RICE PUDDING CRUNCH

POINTS	
per recipe: 14½	per serving: 3½

Ⓥ Serves 4

Preparation time: 10 minutes
Cooking time: 40–45 minutes
Calories per serving: 180
Freezing: not recommended

A childhood favourite, rice pudding is simplicity itself to make and yet is still regarded as an indulgent treat.

FOR THE RICE PUDDING

50 g (1¾ oz) pudding rice

600 ml (1 pint) semi-skimmed milk

25 g (1 oz) caster sugar

a few drops of vanilla essence

400 g can apricot halves in natural juice, drained

FOR THE TOPPING

grated rind of 1 orange

¼ teaspoon mixed spice

50 g (1¾ oz) demerara sugar

15 g (½ oz) chopped almonds

PLUM AND BANANA CRUMBLE

POINTS

per recipe: 25	per serving: 6

 Serves 4

Preparation time: 10 minutes

Cooking time: 40 minutes

Calories per serving: 395

Freezing: not recommended

If you have the Points to spare, serve this favourite with steaming hot ready-to-serve low-fat custard for an extra 2 Points per 150 g (5½ oz).

FOR THE FILLING

600 g (1 lb 5 oz) ripe Victoria plums, halved and stoned

2 large bananas, cut on to 2.5 cm (1-inch) chunks

1 tablespoon light soft brown sugar or caster sugar

FOR THE CRUMBLE

125 g (4½ oz) plain flour

½ teaspoon ground cinnamon or mixed spice

75 g (2¾ oz) half-fat butter

2 tablespoons demerara sugar

50 g (1¾ oz) porridge oats

1 Preheat the oven to Gas Mark 4/ 180°C/350°F.

2 Prepare the filling. Mix the plums, bananas and sugar together. Transfer to a 850 ml (1½-pint) ovenproof dish. Spoon 4 tablespoons of water over the fruit mixture.

3 To make the crumble place the flour, spice, half-fat butter and the sugar in a bowl. Rub together until the mixture resembles coarse breadcrumbs. Stir in the oats.

4 Sprinkle the topping over the fruit, making sure it is completely covered. Transfer to a baking sheet and cook for 40 minutes, or until golden and

bubbling at the edges. Leave to cool slightly before serving.

TOP TIP A food processor makes light work of the crumble mixture. Simply tip all the ingredients into the bowl and process for about 10 seconds .

VARIATION For a change replace the plums with firm pears, peeled and quartered.

Plum and Banana Crumble: Fabulous with ready-to-serve low-fat custard. Add 2 Points.

CREAMY ORANGE PUDDINGS

POINTS

per recipe: 20	per serving: $3^{1}/_{2}$

v *if using free-range eggs*
Serves 6
Preparation time: 15 minutes
Cooking time: 20 minutes
Calories per serving: 190
Freezing: not recommended

Here's a delicious way to boost your winter intake of Vitamin C!

4 medium oranges
low-fat cooking spray
300 g (10½ oz) extra-light low-fat soft cheese
2 large eggs, separated + 1 egg white
75 g (2¾ oz) icing sugar, sieved
1 tablespoon cornflour

1 Preheat the oven to Gas Mark 7/ 220°C/425°F.
2 Finely grate the zest from two of the oranges and set aside. Peel the oranges and use a serrated knife to remove all the bitter white pith, keeping the segments intact. Cut horizontally into 8 mm (¼-inch) slices.
3 Lightly spray the insides of six 125 ml (4 fl oz) basins or small ramekin dishes with the low-fat cooking spray. In a large bowl, beat together the soft cheese, egg yolks, half the icing sugar, cornflour and the orange zest.
4 Whisk the egg whites in a grease-free bowl until stiff, then whisk in the remaining icing sugar. Beat a tablespoon of the meringue mixture into the cream cheese mixture then gently fold in the rest.
5 Arrange the orange slices over the base and sides of each basin then fill with the cheese mixture. Arrange the basins in a roasting dish filled with 2.5 cm (1-inch) water and cover lightly with greaseproof paper. Bake in the preheated oven for 15–20 minutes, or until the filling is still slightly wobbly.
6 Leave to cool for 5 minutes before turning out on to individual serving plates. Serve immediately.

HOT BANANA SOUFFLÉS

POINTS

per recipe: 11	per serving: $2^{1}/_{2}$

v *if using free-range eggs*
Serves 4
Preparation time: 15 minutes
Cooking time: 10 minutes
Calories per serving: 175
Freezing: not recommended

Banana still continues to be the nation's favourite fruit. Try this recipe for the proof of the pudding – a hot and fluffy soufflé which is very easy to make and looks most impressive.

15 g (½ oz) butter, softened
50 g (1¼ oz) caster sugar
3 medium ripe bananas
juice of ½ a lemon
4 egg whites

1 Preheat the oven to Gas Mark 4/ 180°C/350°F. Wipe the inside of four individual ramekin dishes (approximately 9 cm/3½-inch diameter) with the softened butter, then sprinkle with 1 tablespoon sugar, swirling each ramekin until well coated.
2 Liquidise the bananas with half the lemon juice until you have a smooth purée. Set aside.
3 Place the egg whites and a few drops of the remaining lemon juice in a grease-free bowl and whisk to soft peaks. Gradually add the remaining sugar and lemon juice until you have firm white peaks.
4 Whisk one quarter of the egg whites into the banana purée (this helps to loosen the purée), then fold in the remainder carefully.
5 Fill each ramekin with the banana mixture, smoothing over the top. Run your thumb around the inner edge of each ramekin to push the mixture away from the sides.
6 Place on a baking sheet and cook for 8–10 minutes until well risen. Serve immediately.

TOP TIP Ripe bananas are sweeter because more of their starch has been converted to sugar – without changing the Points!

Creamy Orange Pudding: As scrumptious as it looks and only 3½ Points per serving!

Sticky Toffee
Pudding: Low
in Points?
Unbelievable
but true.

STICKY TOFFEE PUDDING

POINTS

per recipe: 31   per serving: 5

Ⓥ *if using free-range eggs*

Serves 6
Preparation time: 10 minutes
Cooking time: 45 minutes
Calories per serving: 355
Freezing: recommended

The recent revival of the good old-fashioned British pudding could tempt even the strongest willed Weight Watchers Member! But there is no need to miss out on scrumptious treats, as this recipe proves.

low-fat cooking spray
175 g (6 oz) stoned dates, chopped
1 teaspoon of bicarbonate of soda
175 g (6 oz) self-raising flour
175 g (6 oz) dark muscovado sugar
50 g (1¾ oz) low-fat spread
3 tablespoons skimmed milk
1 teaspoon vanilla essence
2 medium egg whites, whisked to soft peaks

FOR THE STICKY SAUCE

1 tablespoon dark muscovado sugar
1 tablespoon golden syrup
4 tablespoons virtually-fat-free fromage frais

1 Preheat the oven to Gas Mark 5/190°C/375°F. Spray a 19 cm (7-inch) square cake tin with the low-fat cooking spray and line the base with baking paper.
2 Place the dates in a small pan with 200 ml (7 fl oz) of water. Bring to the boil, then simmer for 5 minutes by which time the dates will have absorbed most of the water. Stir in the bicarbonate of soda.
3 Place the flour, sugar and low-fat spread in a bowl and rub together until the fat has been incorporated into the flour and the mixture is crumbly. Stir in the milk, vanilla essence and dates then fold in the lightly beaten egg whites. Spoon the mixture into the cake tin and level the surface. Bake for 35 minutes or until well risen and firm.
4 To make the sauce, place all the ingredients in a small pan and heat until melted and smooth. Do not allow the mixture to boil.
5 Serve the pudding warm, with a drizzle of the sauce.

VARIATION This pudding is also delicious eaten cold, so save a slice for a day later, to enjoy with a cup of coffee. Serve the pudding as a tea-time cake, if you wish. Dust the surface with sieved icing sugar and add no extra Points.

MAGIC MOCHA PUDDING

POINTS

per recipe: 16   per serving: 2½

Ⓥ *Serves 6*
Preparation time: 10 minutes
Cooking time: 45 minutes
Calories per serving: 165
Freezing: not recommended

This is one of those delightful puddings that results in a light sponge on top concealing a delicious hot mocha sauce inside.

125 g (4½ oz) self-raising flour
40 g (1½ oz) cocoa powder
50 g (1¾ oz) caster sugar
1 teaspoon vanilla essence
125 ml (4 fl oz) semi-skimmed milk

FOR THE MOCHA SAUCE

50 g (1¾ oz) demerara sugar
1 teaspoon instant coffee powder
350 ml (12 fl oz) boiling water

1 Preheat the oven to Gas Mark 4/180°C/350°F.
2 Sieve the flour and 2 level tablespoons of the cocoa powder into a bowl. Stir in the caster sugar, vanilla essence and milk, beating the mixture until smooth. Spread the mixture into a 1.2 litre (2-pint) baking or soufflé dish.
3 Mix the demerara sugar with the remaining cocoa powder and sprinkle it evenly over the creamed mixture. Dissolve the coffee with the boiling water and pour all over the pudding.
4 Bake for 45 minutes until risen and the sponge mixture is firm to the touch. Serve immediately.

APPLE AND GINGER PUDDING

POINTS

per recipe: 22½   per serving: 5½

ⓥ *if using free-range eggs*
Serves 4
Preparation time: 15 minutes
Cooking time: 25 minutes for individual puddings; 40 minutes for a large pudding
Calories per serving: 365
Freezing: recommended

Serve with the sticky sauce on page 45 for a total of 6 Points per serving.

low-fat cooking spray
FOR THE APPLES
2 small dessert apples, peeled, quartered and cut into 5 mm (½-inch) slices

juice of ½ lemon
25 g (1 oz) demerara sugar
15 g (½ oz) low-fat spread
FOR THE SPONGE
125 g (4½ oz) plain flour
½ teaspoon baking powder
½ teaspoon bicarbonate of soda
1 teaspoon ground ginger
25 g (1 oz) soft light brown sugar
1 medium egg, beaten
4 tablespoons milk
4 tablespoons vegetable oil
grated zest of ½ lemon

1 Preheat the oven to Gas Mark 3/ 170°C/325°F. Lightly spray the insides of four individual 175 ml (6 fl oz) bowls or a 600 ml (1-pint) pudding basin with the low-fat cooking spray.
2 Toss the apple slices in a bowl with the lemon juice and demerara sugar. Heat the low-fat spread in a pan and cook the apples until they turn golden and begin to caramelise slightly. Divide the apples between the individual bowls or pudding basin.
3 To make the sponge, sieve the dry ingredients into a bowl. Mix the remaining ingredients in another bowl then add to the dry ingredients, stirring until just combined. Do not over mix.
4 Spoon the sponge mix into the bowls until three-quarters full. Cook the individual puddings for 25 minutes or the larger pudding for 40 minutes or until a skewer inserted in the middle of the puddings comes out clean.

Blackberry Meringue Pudding: A marvelous meringue recipe for only 1½ Points per serving.

BLACKBERRY MERINGUE PUDDING

POINTS

per recipe: 3½   per serving: 1½

ⓥ *if using free-range eggs*
Serves 2
Preparation time: 10 minutes
Cooking time: 15 minutes
Calories per serving: 115
Freezing: not recommended

Here little pots of blackberries are cooked with cinnamon and mallow meringue. An easy recipe for two, or simply scale the ingredients up for more servings.

15 g (½ oz) fresh breadcrumbs
½ teaspoon ground cinnamon
110 g (4 oz) fresh blackberries
1 egg white
40 g (1½ oz) light muscovado or soft brown sugar

1 Preheat the oven to Gas Mark 5/ 190°C/375°F.
2 Heat a small non-stick frying-pan over a low heat and dry-fry the breadcrumbs and cinnamon, stirring occasionally, until toasted and crisp. Remove from the heat and fold through the blackberries.
3 In a small grease-free bowl, whisk the egg white to stiff peaks. Whisk in half the sugar and then fold in the remainder. Fold the blackberry mixture through the meringue and divide between two 8 cm (3-inch) ramekin dishes. Bake for 15 minutes until golden.

VARIATION Replace some of the blackberries with redcurrants or blueberries, or all the fruits with fresh raspberries.

APPLE AND WALNUT PIE

POINTS

per recipe: 31   per serving: 4

(v) *if using free-range eggs*
Serves 8
Preparation time: 15 minutes
Cooking time: 45 minutes
Calories per serving: 240
Freezing: recommended

Hurrah for filo pastry! Low in fat and easy to use, it means that we can enjoy countless favourite pies and flans, without using too many Points.

25 g (1 oz) walnut pieces, toasted
25 g (1 oz) butter
50 g (1³/₄ oz) caster sugar
1 medium egg
grated rind and juice of 1 small lemon
25 g (1 oz) self-raising flour
1 teaspoon ground cinnamon
8 medium crisp eating apples (e.g. Cox's)
270 g pack filo pastry sheets
low-fat cooking spray
icing sugar, to dust

1 Preheat the oven to Gas Mark 5/ 190°C/375°F. Blend the nuts in a food processor until finely chopped. In a small bowl, cream together the butter and 40 g (1½ oz) of sugar. Whisk in the egg and then the lemon rind, flour and ½ teaspoon cinnamon. Finally mix in the nuts.
2 Peel and slice the apples and toss with the remaining sugar, cinnamon and lemon juice.
3 Line a 23 cm (9-inch) flan tin with three-quarters of the filo pastry, allowing the edges to overhang. Spread the nut paste over the base and top with the apples. Gather up the overhanging pastry, scrunching the sheets up like paper. Scrunch up the remaining pastry and use to completely conceal the apple filling.
4 Spray the lid lightly with the low-fat cooking spray and cook for 40–45 minutes. Cover lightly with foil if the pastry browns too much.
5 Serve warm, dusted with some sieved icing sugar.

TOP TIP Handle filo pastry quickly once unrolled as the sheets become dry and brittle after only a short time. Re-package and refrigerate or freeze any unused sheets.

VARIATION Add 1 tablespoon sultanas to the apple filling. Points per serving will be the same.

HOT CHOCOLATE SOUFFLÉ WITH POACHED PEARS

POINTS

per recipe: 25½   per serving: 6½

(v) *if using free-range eggs*
Serves 4
Preparation time: 20 minutes
Cooking time: 35 minutes
Calories per serving: 310
Freezing: not recommended:

Try this for a special dessert.

FOR THE PEARS

150 ml (¹/₄ pint) hot water
25 g (1 oz) caster sugar
2 teaspoons lemon juice
2 medium ripe Comice pears, peeled, cored and each half sliced into 4 wedges

FOR THE SOUFFLÉ

low-fat cooking spray
300 ml (¹/₂ pint) semi-skimmed milk
50 g (1³/₄ oz) dark plain chocolate (minimum 70% cocoa solids), chopped
25 g (1 oz) butter
15 g (¹/₂ oz) plain flour
25 g (1 oz) cornflour
25 g (1 oz) caster sugar
a few drops of vanilla essence
2 large eggs, separated

1 Lightly spray a 20 cm (8-inch) soufflé dish with the low-fat cooking spray.
2 Put the water, sugar and lemon juice in a saucepan, add the pears, cover with a lid and gently poach them for 12–15 minutes, or until completely translucent. Remove from the heat and set aside.
3 Meanwhile make the soufflé. In a small saucepan gently heat half the milk with the chocolate, stirring constantly. When the chocolate has melted, remove from the heat and stir in the remaining milk.
4 Melt the butter in a saucepan, add the flour and cornflour and quickly blend in the chocolate milk. Bring to the boil, stirring constantly, and cook for 1 minute. Remove from the heat and stir in the sugar and vanilla essence.
5 Whisk the egg whites in a grease-free bowl until they form soft peaks. Beat the egg yolks into the chocolate mixture, then fold in the egg whites. Pour the mixture into the soufflé dish, cover with a piece of thick kitchen foil, tying securely with string.
6 Steam over a pan of boiling water for 30 minutes or until just firm to touch.
7 Serve the soufflé with the pear wedges and a little of the reduced poaching juice.

TOP TIP Look out for a minimum content of 70% cocoa solids in the ingredients. This means you can use less for more flavour!

Apple and
Cinnamon
Flapjacks:
Chewy, delicious
oat squares.

teatime treats

The cold nights and chilly winter days bring with them roaring log fires and cosy gatherings over pots of tea – so what could be more appropriate than a slice of moist gingerbread or freshly-made griddle cakes. The tastiest bit about this chapter is that all the recipes are low Point equivalents of your favourite teatime treats!

APPLE AND CINNAMON FLAPJACKS

POINTS

per recipe: 30   per slice: 2¹/₂

(V) *Makes 12 squares*
Preparation time: 10 minutes
Cooking time: 15 minutes
Calories per square: 145
Freezing: recommended

These little bites are great for breakfast on the move, the lunch box or to just sit and nibble at leisure!

100 g (3¹/₂ oz) low-fat spread, melted

75 g (2³/₄ oz) dark muscovado sugar

2 tablespoons golden syrup

175 g (6 oz) porridge oats

1 teaspoon ground cinnamon

75 g (2³/₄ oz) dried apple pieces, chopped into bite-size pieces

25 g (1 oz) raisins or currants

1 Preheat the oven to Gas Mark 5/ 190°C/375°F.
2 Heat together the low-fat spread, sugar and syrup until melted and well blended.
3 Mix in the oats, cinnamon, apple pieces and raisins or currants.
4 Spread in an 18 cm (7-inch) shallow square tin. Bake for 15 minutes. Leave to cool in the tin before marking into 12 squares. Once completely cold, remove from the tin and store in an airtight container.

TOP TIP Measure out syrup using a hot metal spoon if you require 'tablespoons', or by placing the tin of syrup on to the scales and subtracting the required amount from the starting weight as you spoon out the syrup.

VARIATION Dried apple can be found in health-food shops and most supermarkets alongside the baking section. Replace the apple with 50 g (1³/₄ oz) mixed dried fruit. Allow 2½ Points per square.

1 Preheat the oven to Gas Mark 4/ 180°C/350°F. Line the base and sides of a 23 cm (9-inch) round loose-bottomed cake tin with greaseproof paper. Smear the paper with the butter, and then sprinkle 1 tablespoon granulated sugar evenly over the base and sides of the tin. Mix the remainder with the cranberries and nuts and scatter over the base of the tin.

2 To make the cake, sieve together the flour, cocoa powder, baking powder and spice in a bowl. Whisk the eggs and sugar together in a bowl set over a pan of simmering water. Keep whisking until a trail is left on the surface from the beaters.

3 Fold in the flour in batches, taking care not to knock the air out of the egg mixture. Finally, trickle and fold in the oil.

4 Pour the cake mixture into the tin. Place on a baking sheet and bake for 40 minutes or until the cake is springy to the touch and a skewer inserted in the centre comes out clean. Cool for 10 minutes before turning the cake out on to a cooling rack and removing the paper lining.

TOP TIP It is important to spend the time whisking the eggs and sugar until the mixture is really mousse-like and foamy.

VARIATION For an Orange and Cranberry Spiced Slice, replace the cocoa powder with its weight in flour, and add the grated zest of 1 large orange with the eggs and sugar. Drizzle the juice of the orange over the skewered cake once cooked. Points remain the same. Serve warm.

Cranberry Spiced Slice: One slice of this stunning cake is only 3½ Points.

CRANBERRY SPICED SLICE

POINTS

per recipe: 34½   per slice: 3½

Ⓥ   *if using free-range eggs*
Makes 10 slices
Preparation time: 20 minutes
Cooking time: 40 minutes
Calories per slice: 190
Freezing: recommended

Cranberries start to appear in the shops towards the end of November. Make the most of this shiny red berry – there's more to it than cranberry sauce! Delicious with a cup of freshly brewed coffee.

FOR THE TOPPING

25 g (1 oz) butter
75 g (2¾ oz) granulated sugar
250 g (9 oz) fresh cranberries
50 g (1¾ oz) pecan nuts or walnuts, chopped coarsely

FOR THE CAKE

75 g (2¾ oz) self-raising flour
2 tablespoons cocoa powder
¼ teaspoon baking powder
½ teaspoon ground allspice
3 medium eggs
75 g (2¾ oz) caster sugar
1 tablespoon vegetable oil

RICH DARK FRUIT CAKE

POINTS

per recipe: 61   per slice: 3

V *if using free-range eggs*

Makes 20 slices

Preparation time: 25 minutes

Cooking time: 1³/₄ hours

Calories per slice: 275

Freezing: recommended

We all have a favourite rich fruit cake recipe – often handed down through the generations. But at times when we want to have that special celebration cake without the high fat content, isn't it great to have an alternative recipe which means you can stick to tradition without it sticking to the hips!

350 g (12 oz) ready-to-eat prunes

6 tablespoons brandy or sherry

finely grated zest and juice of 1 large lemon

finely grated zest and juice of 1 large orange

200 g (7 oz) dark muscovado sugar

4 medium eggs

1 tablespoon black treacle

1 medium cooking apple, peeled and grated

350 g (12 oz) plain flour

2 teaspoons baking powder

2 teaspoons mixed spice

¹/₂ teaspoon ground nutmeg

800 g (1 lb 12 oz) luxury dried mixed fruits

6 tablespoons semi-skimmed milk

1 Heat the oven to Gas Mark 4/ 180°C/350°F. Line a deep 23 cm (9-inch) round cake tin with greaseproof or parchment paper.

2 Purée the prunes in a food processor or liquidiser, together with the brandy or sherry, lemon and

orange zest and juice. Transfer to a bowl and whisk in the sugar and eggs until the mixture becomes light and fluffy. Whisk in the treacle.

3 Use a metal spoon to stir in the apple, flour, baking powder and spices. Finally mix in the dried fruit and enough milk to form a soft dropping consistency. Transfer to the prepared tin, levelling out the surface.

4 Bake in the centre of the oven for 45 minutes, then reduce the oven temperature to Gas Mark 3/ 170°C/325°F and continue to cook for 1 hour or until the cake is well risen and a skewer inserted in the centre comes out clean.

5 Leave the cake to cool in the tin before removing and discarding the paper. Wrap the cake in fresh paper or foil and store in an airtight tin. The cake is best left for at least a day to mature before cutting.

TOP TIP An old wives' tale or not, I always leave a whole apple in the storage container alongside my fruit cakes to help keep them moist.

VARIATION To decorate the cake, brush the surface with 1 tablespoon apricot jam and roll out 175 g (6 oz) ready-prepared icing. Press firmly on to the cake, trim the edges and decorate with strips of lemon or orange rind. This will add ¹/₂ Point per slice.

Rich Dark Fruit Cake: Who says you can't enjoy Christmas treats and lose weight too?

Griddle Cakes with Banana Jam: Indulge yourself!

GRIDDLE CAKES WITH BANANA JAM

POINTS

per recipe: 23   **per cake: 1½**

V *if using a free-range egg*
Makes 16
Preparation time: 20 minutes
Cooking time: 15 minutes
Calories per serving: 85
Freezing: not recommended

FOR THE GRIDDLE CAKES

100 g (3½ oz) self-raising flour

a pinch of salt

1 medium egg

1 tablespoon treacle

150 ml (¼ pint) skimmed milk

15 g (½ oz) butter

FOR THE BANANA JAM

200 ml (7 fl oz) fresh apple juice

a stick of cinnamon, broken in half

2 cloves

5 cm (2-inch) strip of pared lemon rind

1 tablespoon lemon juice

1 tablespoon dark muscovado sugar

4 medium ripe bananas

15 g (½ oz) butter

1 First make the batter. Sift the flour and salt into a bowl. Make a well in the centre and break in the egg. Add the treacle and milk and work in the flour to make a smooth batter. Leave to stand for 10 minutes. Make the banana jam.

2 Heat the fruit juice with the cinnamon, cloves, lemon rind, juice and sugar. Boil rapidly to reduce to 6 tablespoons. Strain into a bowl,

add the bananas and mash to a smooth purée. Beat in the butter.

3 Heat a heavy-based frying-pan and rub some of the butter over the surface. Use a ladle to pour on small mounds of batter, spacing well apart. As soon as the cakes are bubbling, turn them over with a palette knife and cook until set and golden brown on the other side. Keep the batches warm in a folded clean tea towel until all the mixture has been cooked.

4 Serve the griddle cakes with the banana jam.

GOLDEN PUMPKIN TRAYBAKE

POINTS

per recipe: 40   **per slice: 3½**

V *if using free-range eggs*
Makes 12
Preparation time: 30 minutes + soaking
Cooking time: 30–35 minutes
Calories per square: 220
Freezing: recommended

40 g (1½ oz) dried apricots

250 g (9 oz) pumpkin or squash, cooked

low-fat cooking spray

225 g (8 oz) self-raising flour

1 teaspoon ground cinnamon (optional)

grated rind of 1 orange

200 g (7 oz) caster sugar

2 medium eggs, beaten

4 tablespoons vegetable oil

FOR THE ICING

75 g (2¾ oz) icing sugar

2 teaspoons fresh orange juice

1 Cover the apricots with boiling water and leave to plump up for 30 minutes. Drain, reserving 2 tablespoons of the liquid.

2 Purée together the pumpkin or squash and the apricots to make 300 ml (10 fl oz) of purée, adding the reserved water, if necessary.

3 Preheat the oven to Gas Mark 4/ 180°C/350F°. Lightly spray and base line a 28 × 18 cm (11 × 7-inch) tin.

4 Place the flour, cinnamon, if using, orange rind and sugar in a bowl and make a well in the centre. Add the eggs, oil and purée and mix just enough to combine all the ingredients. Pour into the cake tin, levelling out the surface.

5 Bake for 30–35 minutes, until firm to the touch. Leave to cool in the tin.

6 Meanwhile, make the icing. Mix together the icing sugar with just enough orange juice to make an icing that drizzles off the spoon. Using a teaspoon, drizzle the icing across the sponge surface. Leave to set before cutting into 12 pieces.

CARROT AND SULTANA CAKE

POINTS

per recipe: 36	per slice: 3½

Ⓥ *if using free-range eggs*
Makes 10 slices
Preparation time: 15 minutes
Cooking time: 55–65 minutes
Calories per serving: 220
Freezing: recommended for the cake only

Great for keeping (if it lasts that long!).

low-fat cooking spray
225 g (8 oz) plain flour
1 teaspoon baking powder
1 teaspoon bicarbonate of soda
1 teaspoon mixed spice
1 teaspoon salt
2 medium eggs, beaten
50 g (1¾ oz) dark muscovado sugar
3 tablespoons vegetable oil
2 tablespoons semi-skimmed milk
juice of 1 large orange

300 g (10 oz) carrots, grated
50 g (1¾ oz) sultanas

FOR THE FROSTING

225 g (8 oz) extra-light low-fat soft cheese (e.g. Kraft Philadelphia Light)
75 g (2¾ oz) virtually-fat-free fromage frais
4 tablespoons icing sugar, sifted
zest of 1 orange

1 Preheat the oven to Gas Mark 4/ 180°C/350°F. Spray and line a 20.5 cm (8-inch) round loose-bottomed cake tin with parchment or greaseproof paper

2 Sift the flour, baking powder and bicarbonate of soda, mixed spice and salt into a mixing bowl. Make a well in the centre. Beat together the eggs, sugar, oil, milk and orange juice, and pour into the centre. Mix together well to form a smooth batter. Beat in the carrots and sultanas.

3 Spoon the mixture into the tin. Bake for 55–65 minutes until a

Carrot and Sultana Cake: Ideal for a break at work with a cup of tea.

skewer comes out clean. Cool in the tin.

4 To make the frosting, beat the soft cheese with the fromage frais until soft and smooth. Beat in the icing sugar and the orange zest. Remove the cake from the tin and decorate with the frosting.

ORCHARD FRUIT AND GINGER TEA BREAD

POINTS

per recipe: 26	per slice: 2

Ⓥ *if using free-range eggs*
Makes 12 slices
Preparation time: 10 minutes + soaking
Cooking time: 55–60 minutes
Calories per slice: 155
Freezing: recommended

Perfect for the lunchbox and for the freezer.

125 g (4½ oz) dried pears, chopped roughly
125 g (4½ oz) dried apples, chopped roughly
300 ml (½ pint) strong tea

225 g (8 oz) plain flour
2 teaspoons ground ginger
2 teaspoons baking powder
100 g (3½ oz) dark muscovado sugar
1 medium egg, beaten
25 g (1 oz) stem ginger, chopped

1 Cover the dried chopped fruit with the tea and leave to soak for 2 hours. Line a 900 g (2 lb) loaf tin with greaseproof or parchment paper.

2 Preheat the oven to Gas Mark 5/ 190°C/375°F. Place all the ingredients in a large bowl and mix thoroughly. Turn into the prepared tin and level the surface. Bake for 55–60 minutes until firm. (Cover with a piece of greaseproof paper during cooking if the surface of the cake browns too quickly.)

3 Leave the cake to cool in the tin for 10 minutes before transferring to a wire rack.

TOP TIP Look out for the wide variety of dried fruits now available. Do not be tempted to nibble at them as they are still quite high in calories. However, they are virtually fat-free, naturally sweet and flavoursome, so make an excellent cooking ingredient.

VARIATION Replace the apples with 3 dried apricots and soak the fruit in 300 ml (½ pint) orange juice. This will be 2 Points per slice.

Christmas Mincemeat Filo Slices: Relax and enjoy the season with these 3 Point slices!

Entertaining around meal times and special occasions can be a fraught time for Weight Watchers Members but meals are controllable and Points can be carefully counted. As inviting as they sound, a Christmas drinks party, a birthday gathering or a family get-together can make counting the Points difficult.

Knowing how much we all enjoy food, this chapter encourages you to plan for those special occasions. You will find lots of quick, easy, tasty and appetising ideas for party food. Before these occasions, fill yourself up with Point free vegetables or a cup of soup to take the edge off your appetite, as generally they are held when you are at your hungriest!

CHRISTMAS MINCEMEAT FILO SLICES

POINTS

per recipe: 48½   per serving: 3

Ⓥ if using vegetarian mincemeat
Makes 16 slices
Preparation time: 20 minutes
Cooking time: 35 minutes
Calories per serving: 185
Freezing: recommended

There is no reason why we can't offer family and visiting friends festive fare over the holidays. Try these delicious, but easy, crisp flaky slices – a variation on mince pies which have all the usual delicious flavours but without the usual Points! Serve with brandy butter, adding 1½ Points per heaped teaspoon.

50 g (1¾ oz) walnuts, chopped
100 g (3½ oz) fresh brown breadcrumbs
50 g (1¾ oz) light muscovado sugar
400 g jar traditional mincemeat
2 medium dessert apples, peeled, cored and chopped
175 g (6 oz) cranberries
grated rind of 1 medium orange
50 g (1¾ oz) half-fat butter, melted
270 g pack filo pastry, thawed
icing sugar, for dusting

1 Preheat the oven to Gas Mark 5/ 190°C/375°F.
2 Mix together the nuts, breadcrumbs and sugar. Line the grill pan with foil, and spread the mixture out over the pan. Cook under a preheated grill for 2–3 minutes, stirring from time to time until the crumbs are toasted. Leave to cool.
3 Mix together the mincemeat, apples, cranberries and orange rind. Stir in the crumb mixture. Lightly brush a 23 × 33 cm (9 × 13-inch) Swiss roll tin with the melted butter. Layer three sheets of filo in the base, then spread with half the mincemeat mixture. Arrange three more pastry layers on top, spread the remaining mincemeat on top and finally cover with the remaining pastry. Brush the top with the remaining butter. Use a sharp knife to trim around the inside edge of the tin, discarding any overhanging pastry.

4 Bake for 35 minutes or until the pastry is crisp and golden. Cool in the tin before dusting with icing sugar and cutting into 16 slices. This is best served at room temperature.

TOP TIP Read labels carefully on food. Now that there are so many varieties of mincemeat available at Christmas, it is not surprising that very often the fat and calorie content go up with the price! Buy a traditional recipe that offers fewest Points and check whether it contains animal suet if you wish to cook a vegetarian version.

CAMPFIRE CASSEROLE

POINTS

per recipe: 19   per serving: 4½

Serves 4
Preparation time: 10 minutes
Cooking time: 30 minutes
Calories per serving: 370
Freezing: recommended

Perfect for Guy Fawkes Night, this is a hearty 'Bangers 'n' Beans' campfire supper – the kids will love it. Make it in one pan and, if you can, set up a stove to keep it warm outside and serve accompanied by a medium slice of crusty white bread adding 1 Point.

1 tablespoon sunflower oil
450 g (1 lb) 95% fat-free pork sausages, cut into thick slices
1 large onion, finely chopped
450 g (1 lb) potatoes, peeled and cut into 2.5 cm (1-inch) chunks
3 large carrots, cut into 2.5 cm (1-inch) chunks
300 ml (½ pint) hot chicken stock
230 g can chopped tomatoes
1 tablespoon Worcestershire sauce
415 g can Weight Watchers From Heinz baked beans
salt and freshly ground black pepper

1 Heat the oil in a large pan, add the sausages and cook for 8–10 minutes, stirring occasionally until evenly browned.
2 Add the onion, potatoes and carrots to the pan and cook for a further 5 minutes.
3 Stir in the hot stock, tomatoes and Worcestershire sauce. Bring to the boil, then reduce the heat, cover and simmer for 10–15 minutes or until the vegetables are just tender. Stir in the baked beans and heat through for a further minute. Season to taste.
4 Ladle into warm bowls and serve.

TOP TIP If you have a slow cooker, prepare the casserole in the kitchen then transfer it to the slow cooker to keep warm until required, perhaps moving it to a more convenient location like the garage. It will not spoil or burn (unlike the poor old Guy).

VARIATION For a curried casserole, add 1 teaspoon curry powder with the vegetables at step 2.

BUBBLE AND SQUEAK PATTIES

POINTS

per recipe: 13   per serving: 3

Serves 4
Preparation time: 20 minutes
Cooking time: 10 minutes
Calories per serving: 265
Freezing: not recommended

It is hard to decide which I prefer – the festive treats on Christmas Day, or the rich pickings a day or so later! Here is a well-known and tasty way of using up left-overs.

Accompany with cranberry sauce or pickles and extra vegetables or a salad adding Points as necessary.

450 g (1 lb) potatoes
175 g (6 oz) cooked Brussels sprouts or winter greens, shredded
175 g (6 oz) cooked turkey meat, diced
75 g (2¾ oz) cooked ham, diced
2 tablespoons seasoned flour
1 tablespoon vegetable oil
salt and freshly ground black pepper

1 Peel and cook the potatoes in lightly salted boiling water for 15–20 minutes until tender. Drain and mash.
2 Mix the vegetables, turkey and ham into the mash. Season and shape into 8 patties. Dust in the seasoned flour.
3 Heat half the oil in a large non-stick frying-pan and fry patties for 4–5 minutes on each side until golden brown. Do this in two batches, using the remaining oil, as required.
4 Serve 2 patties per person.

TOP TIP Cooked turkey will keep in the refrigerator for three or four days, but it is a good idea to strip the carcass and freeze the meat in handy portions – either sliced and layered between clingfilm or diced and tied in a freezer bag ready for a quick curry. Boil up the carcass for a delicious stock base for a soup. The stock will freeze for up to 3 months.

TASTY TOPPED BLINIS

POINTS

per recipe: 9½   per serving: 1

Makes 16 blinis (serves 8)
Preparation time: 10 minutes
Calories per blini with either
topping: 35
Freezing: not recommended

Nibbles and party food have to be quick to make and definitely hassle-free, otherwise the whole purpose of entertaining friends becomes stressful and a chore. Even strong wills can weaken at times like this! So try these little low Point pancakes, crowned with tasty toppings.

135 g pack Blinis (Russian-style pancakes)

FOR THE SMOKED SALMON AND HORSERADISH TOPPING

1 tablespoon horseradish relish
1 tablespoon 0% fat Greek-style yogurt
1 small cooked beetroot, chopped
75 g (2¾ oz) smoked salmon trimmings
freshly ground black pepper
snipped fresh chives, to garnish

FOR THE TURKEY AND TOMATO TOPPING

2 tablespoons half-fat crème fraîche
1 tablespoon tomato or onion relish
3-4 wafer thin slices smoked turkey, cut into pieces
flat leaf parsley, to garnish

1 Warm the blinis through under a low grill setting, just to refresh them.
2 To assemble the smoked salmon blinis, mix together the horseradish and yogurt. Spread a little over each blini, top with some beetroot and finally a folded piece of salmon. Garnish with the snipped chives and pepper.
3 To make the turkey blinis, spoon some creme fraîchè on to each blini, then a dollop of relish followed by the turkey. Garnish with a tiny sprig of parsley.
4 Serve, allowing one of each per portion.

TOP TIP Blinis are little Russian-style pancakes and are available at supermarkets ready-made. You can also use little toasts or slices of baguette as an alternative. Or

use a small pitta bread, split in half then cut into 10 pieces and baked until crisp. Adjust the Points accordingly.

VARIATION Relishes and pickle tend to be quite low-fat, so experiment with different flavours.

Tasty Topped Blinis: Ideal for a party at only 1 Point per serving!

YULETIDE YOGURT

POINTS

per recipe: 10   per serving: 5

ⓥ *if using vegetarian Christmas pudding*
Serves 2
Preparation time: 10 minutes + 1 hour chilling
Calories per serving: 300
Freezing: not recommended

Here is a novel way of getting that second helping of Christmas pudding.

A little goes a long way with this fruity snack – ideal as a brunch too. Make an hour or so before you need it to give the sugar topping time to dissolve into a sweet glaze.

75 g (2¾ oz) leftover, cooked Christmas pudding, cold and crumbled
2 small satsumas
1 medium banana, sliced
75 g (2¾ oz) seedless grapes, halved
150 g (5 fl oz) low-fat plain yogurt
1 tablespoon half-fat crème fraîche
3 teaspoons dark muscovado sugar

1 Put the crumbled pudding in a bowl. One at a time, hold the satsumas over the bowl to peel and segment them – allowing any juice to soak into the pudding. Chop the flesh and add it to the pudding together with the banana and grapes.
2 Mix together the yogurt and crème fraîche. Carefully fold through the fruit mixture. Divide between two glass dishes. Sprinkle on the sugar, cover and chill for 1 hour.

BABY POTATO BITES

POINTS

per potato half with topping: 1

Makes 16 mini potato halves
Preparation time: 15 minutes
Cooking time: 30–40 minutes
Calories per potato half: with all
toppings 35 except Crème Fraîche
and Chilli Topping which is 30

8 small potatoes (e.g. Charlotte)

2 tablespoons olive oil

coarse ground salt and black pepper

FOR THE CORONATION CHICKEN TOPPING

25 g (1 oz) cooked chicken, chopped

1 tablespoon chopped red pepper

2 tablespoons virtually-fat-free fromage frais

1 teaspoon curry paste

1 teaspoon mango chutney

chopped fresh parsley, to garnish

FOR THE CRÈME FRAÎCHE AND CHILLI TOPPING

2 tablespoons half-fat crème fraîche

1 teaspoon finely chopped green chilli

1 spring onion, chopped finely

FOR THE PRAWN AND TOMATO SALSA TOPPING

2 tablespoons 95% fat-free fresh tomato salsa

8 cooked prawns

4 tiny sprigs of fresh coriander

1 Preheat the oven to Gas Mark 5/ 190°C/375°F. Toss eight small potatoes in the oil and tip into a shallow roasting pan. Sprinkle with salt and pepper and roast for 30–40 minutes until tender. Leave until cool enough to handle.

2 Meanwhile make up the toppings –

each is sufficient for four potato halves. Simply combine the ingredients together for each option, leaving some chopped herbs to garnish.

3 Cut the potatoes in half and then top the warm potatoes with your choice of topping(s). Arrange on a plate and serve immediately.

TOP TIP The potatoes can be cooked up to 2 hours ahead. Do not cut them in half until needed. Cool, cover and keep in the refrigerator. Either warm up before serving or serve them at room temperature.

VARIATION Try a Blue Cheese and Chive Topping for 1½ Points per potato half. Mix together 25 g (1 oz) blue cheese, 1 tablespoon half-fat crème fraîche and 1 teaspoon chopped chives.

SPICY POTATO WEDGES WITH A COOLING DIP

POINTS

per recipe: 19   per serving: 2

Ⓥ *Makes 36 wedges (serves 9)*
Preparation time: 10 minutes
Cooking time: 45–50 minutes
Calories per serving (4 wedges): 155
Freezing: recommended for the wedges only

These can be served as a snack with grilled chicken or cold meats and salad.

FOR THE POTATO WEDGES

6 medium potatoes (approximately 175 g/6 oz each), washed and cut into 6 wedges

4 tablespoons tomato purée

juice of 1 lemon

3 teaspoons ground coriander

2 teaspoons ground cumin

1 teaspoon chilli powder

2 tablespoons vegetable oil

½ teaspoon salt

fresh coriander sprigs, to garnish

FOR THE DIP

150 ml (5 fl oz) 0% fat Greek-style yogurt

2 tablespoons half-fat crème fraîche

2 spring onions, chopped finely

zest and juice of 1 lime

salt, to taste

2 tablespoons chopped finely coriander, to garnish

1 Preheat the oven to Gas Mark 6/ 200°C/400°F.

2 Put all the ingredients, except the potatoes, in a bowl and whisk together to form a smooth paste.

Add the potatoes and shake gently until the wedges are well covered.

3 Arrange the potato wedges in one layer in a roasting dish and cook for 45–50 minutes until golden and crisp.

4 Meanwhile make the dip. Mix together all the ingredients and spoon into a bowl. Chill until required.

5 Carefully remove the cooked wedges from the tray to a serving platter leaving a space in the centre for the dip bowl. Garnish with fresh coriander sprigs.

TOP TIP The wedges can be prepared up to a day ahead of serving and kept refrigerated until required. Simply re-heat in a hot oven (Gas Mark 7/220°C/425°F) for 10 minutes.

Baby Potato Bites: Fabulous tasting fuss-free canapés which look impressive too!

PARMESAN POLENTA CAKES WITH GRILLED VEGETABLES

POINTS

per recipe: 19½   per serving: 1½

Ⓥ *Makes 15*

Preparation time: 15 minutes + cooling

Cooking time: 15 minutes

Calories per cake: 85

Freezing: not recommended

Enter into the party spirit without any worries at all!

FOR THE POLENTA CAKES

225 g (8 oz) instant (quick cook) polenta

25 g (1 oz) parmesan cheese, finely grated

1 teaspoon each finely chopped fresh parsley and chives

salt and freshly ground black pepper

FOR THE VEGETABLE TOPPING

15 small cherry tomatoes

2 medium courgettes, cut diagonally into fifteen 5 mm (¼-inch) slices

½ medium yellow pepper, de-seeded

low-fat cooking spray

FOR THE GARNISH

2 tablespoons extra-virgin olive oil

15 small basil leaves

freshly ground black pepper

1 Bring 1.2 litres (2 pints) salted water to the boil in a large pan. Pour in the polenta in a steady stream, whisking well so lumps do not form. Cook over a very gentle heat for 5 minutes until smooth. Stir in the parmesan, parsley and chives, and season with salt and black pepper. Turn into a 25 × 16.5 cm (10 × 6½-inch) shallow tin, levelling out the surface. Leave to cool.

2 Preheat the grill, line the grill tray with foil and spray with the low-fat cooking spray. Cut the polenta into 15 squares. Transfer to the grill pan and grill for 5 minutes on each side.

3 Meanwhile prepare the vegetables. Make a cross in the top of each tomato, as you would a Brussels sprout. Preheat the grill and arrange the vegetables in the grill pan. Spray with the low-fat cooking spray and cook under a hot grill for 5 minutes or until they soften and become singed around the edges. Turn the courgette slices and the pepper over half way through cooking.

4 Arrange the cooked polenta squares on to a serving platter and top each with a disc of courgette and a whole tomato. Press with a fork to lightly crush the tomato. Cut the pepper into narrow strips and arrange decoratively over the top of each cake. Finally, drizzle with a little oil and garnish with a whole basil leaf. Grind on plenty of black pepper. Serve 15 guests with a smile!

TOP TIP Polenta is a popular staple diet in northern Italy and is now widely available in our supermarkets.

VARIATION They are endless! Top with mushrooms, parma ham, tuna fish, onions, a thick tomato sauce, or cheese.

TOFFEE APPLE WEDGES

POINTS

per recipe: 21½   per wedge: 1

Ⓥ *Makes 24 wedges*

Preparation time: 15 minutes

Cooking time: 15 minutes

Calories per wedge: 55

Freezing: not recommended

A special treat to pass around to friends.

4 medium dessert apples, cored and quartered

225 g (8 oz) demerara sugar

1 tablespoon golden syrup

25 g (1 oz) butter

2 teaspoons lemon juice

2 tablespoons water

1 Line two baking trays with non-stick parchment. Prepare the apples. Have to hand some long handled tongs.

2 Place the sugar, syrup, butter, lemon juice and water in a heavy-based saucepan and stir over a gentle heat until the sugar has dissolved.

3 Bring to the boil and boil rapidly without stirring for 5–10 minutes or until half a teaspoon of the mixture becomes hard and brittle when dropped into a bowl of cold water. (Take care to remove the pan from the heat before testing.)

4 Using the tongs, place half the apple wedges into the pan of toffee, making sure they are well coated. Remove, allowing the excess toffee to drip away. Spread the apples out on to the non-stick parchment. Repeat with the remaining wedges.

5 Leave to set in a cool dry place until serving. If wished, wrap each wedge in a piece of cellophane.

TOP TIP Take great care when making toffee as it gets extremely hot. Keep young children out of the way and supervise any older children who may wish to help.

Toffee Apple Wedges: Yummy toffee-coated apple slices and only 1 Point each!

1 Preheat the oven to Gas Mark 4/ 180°C/350°F. Line a muffin tray with twelve paper muffin cases. Place the cranberries, mincemeat and apple in a bowl. Mix together well.

2 Sift the flour, baking powder, spices, sugar and salt in a separate bowl. Put the egg, milk and oil in a jug and whisk together well.

3 Make a well in the centre of the dry ingredients and pour in the egg mixture quickly mixing together until just blended. Do not over-mix.

4 Carefully fold in the fruit mixture. Divide between twelve muffin cases. Bake for 20−25 minutes until well risen and golden. Transfer to a wire rack to cool slightly before serving.

TOP TIP If you over-mix any muffin mixture, the muffins will become tough, so handle with care!

VARIATIONS Replace the cranberries with 1 medium banana, chopped. Allow 3 Points per muffin.

Replace the mincemeat with 75 g (2¾ oz) chopped ready-to-eat apricots. Allow 3 Points per muffin.

Boxing Day Muffins: A warming winter treat for breakfast or teatime.

BOXING DAY MUFFINS

POINTS

per recipe: 32½   per muffin: 3

Ⓥ   *if using vegetarian mincemeat and free-range eggs*

Makes: 12
Preparation time: 15 minutes
Cooking time: 25 minutes
Calories per serving: 180
Freezing: recommended

A great way to start the day is with these muffins – warm and freshly made – and a mug of home-brewed coffee. They will set you up for a traditional Boxing Day walk!

110 g (4 oz) fresh cranberries
100 g (3½ oz) mincemeat
1 small apple, peeled, cored and grated
300 g (10½ oz) plain flour
1 teaspoon baking powder
1 teaspoon mixed spice
1 teaspoon ground cinnamon
50 g (1¾ oz) light muscovado sugar
a pinch of salt
1 medium egg, beaten
200 ml (7 fl oz) skimmed milk
3 tablespoons vegetable oil

DELICIOUS CHEESEY DIP

POINTS

per recipe: 7   per serving: $^1/_2$

Serves 12
Preparation time: 15 minutes
Calories per serving: 30
Freezing: not recommended

Dips are easy to whip up and they offer a relaxed style of nibbling! This creamy dip is especially low in fat, and the great bonus is that huge pile of crisp crunchy vegetables – endless free Points to distract you from anything else within sight!

200 g pack 95% fat-free soft cheese
150 g carton 0% fat Greek-style yogurt
2 teaspoons Dijon mustard
2 teaspoons chopped fresh chives
50 g (1³/₄ oz) wafer-thin smoked ham, shredded
salt and freshly ground black pepper
assorted vegetables i.e cauliflower florets, radishes, celery, peppers, spring onions, carrots, cucumber, cherry tomatoes, button mushrooms

1 Make the dip a couple of hours ahead of time to give the flavours a chance to develop. Simply mix together the cream cheese, yogurt, mustard and chives. Season well, then fold in the ham. Cover and chill until required.
2 Prepare the vegetables up to an hour before you need them. Wash and trim the vegetables into bite-sized 'dippers'. Transfer to the fridge. They will become refreshingly crisp for serving.
3 To serve, place the bowl of dip in the centre of a large platter, and arrange the vegetable crudités around the edge.

TOP TIP A secret store of crisp vegetable crudités is well worth having in the fridge to nibble on every time you open that door!

VARIATIONS There are so many variations and options for making low Point dips. For a vegetarian dip try this colourful one: replace the ham with 2 small cooked beetroot, finely chopped and mixed in with the chives. Use horseradish relish instead of mustard if preferred. This dip will have ½ Point per serving.

SPICED CRANBERRY AND ORANGE WARMER

POINTS

per recipe: 12   per serving: 2

 Serves 6
Preparation time: 5 minutes
Cooking time: 5 minutes + 5 minutes standing
Calories per serving: 135
Freezing: not recommended

This fruity drink, suitable for all the family, will surely bring inner warmth to a chilly winters night.

1 litre (1³/₄ pints) cranberry juice
300 ml (½ pint) freshly squeezed orange juice
2 cloves
1 cinnamon stick (approximately 5 cm/2-inches)
2 teaspoons demerara sugar
1 orange, halved and cut into slices

1 Place all the ingredients except the sliced orange in a saucepan. Heat gently for 5 minutes without letting the liquid boil. Switch off the heat and leave to stand for 5 minutes.
2 Carefully strain into a large heatproof jug, add the orange slices and serve in heatproof glasses or tumblers.

TOP TIP If you have a slow cooker, transfer the heated juice, with the spices, to the preheated pot. It will keep warm for several hours without spoiling. Simply ladle out as required.

VARIATION This is a great non-alcoholic drink, but for a special glow why not add 2 teaspoons brandy per glass? Allow 2½ Points per serving.

A

apples: apple and cinnamon flapjacks — 49
    apple and ginger pudding — 46
    apple and walnut pie — 47
    toffee apple wedges — 60
apricot and almond rice pudding crunch — 40
aubergine, tomato and mozzarella bake — 31

B

bakes: aubergine, tomato and mozzarella
    bake — 31
    root vegetable bake — 34
bananas: hot banana soufflés — 42
    plum and banana crumble — 41
    griddle cakes with banana jam — 52
beef: beef in beer with dumplings — 27
    potato-topped chilli beef — 29
blackberry meringue pudding — 46
blinis, tasty topped — 57
bread pudding, cheese, onion and tomato — 32
broccoli soup, butterbean and — 13
bubble and squeak patties — 56

C

cakes: carrot and sultana cake — 53
    rich dark fruit cake — 51
casseroles: braised pork casserole — 26
    campfire casserole — 56
    chicken casserole with orange and
      cinnamon — 16
    chicken hotpot — 15
    sausage and lentil casserole — 22
cheese: spinach, egg and cheese ramekins — 36
    cheese, onion and tomato bread pudding — 32
    delicious cheesey dip — 63
chicken: chicken casserole with orange
    and cinnamon — 16
    chicken hotpot — 15
    chicken and ham pancake pie — 17
    farmhouse chicken and vegetable broth — 9
chick-peas, hot spiced — 37
Chinese-style lamb — 26
chocolate:
    hot chocolate soufflé with poached pears — 47
    magic mocha pudding — 45
    steamed chocolate castles — 38
Christmas mincemeat filo slices — 55
cranberries: cranberry spiced slice — 50
    spiced cranberry and orange warmer — 63
creamy orange puddings — 42
crumbles: mushroom and leek crumble — 35
    plum and banana crumble — 41
curry, stir-fry prawn — 18

E

egg and cheese ramekins, spinach, — 36

F

farmhouse chicken and vegetable broth — 9
fish: fisherman's catch — 10
    fish pie — 21
    spicy fish casserole — 20
    winter seafood stew — 21
flapjacks, apple and cinnamon — 49
fruit and ginger tea bread, orchard — 53
fruit cake, rich dark — 51

G

ginger: orchard fruit and ginger tea bread — 53
goulash with pasta, meatball — 24
griddle cakes with banana jam — 52

H

ham: chicken and ham pancake pie — 17
    roast ham with spicy plum glaze — 28

I

Irish stew — 25

K

korma, winter vegetable — 37

L

lamb: Chinese-style lamb — 26
    roasted lamb steaks — 29
lentil casserole, sausage and — 22

M

marrow, baked feta and tomato — 35
meatball goulash with pasta — 24
meringue pudding, blackberry — 46
mocha pudding, magic — 45
muffins, Boxing day — 62
mushrooms: chicken and ham pancake pie — 17
    mushroom and leek crumble — 35

O

onion soup, golden — 7
orange puddings, creamy — 42

P

parmesan polenta cakes with grilled
    vegetables — 60
pie, apple and walnut — 47
pie, fish — 21
plum and banana crumble — 41
polenta cakes, parmesan, with grilled
    vegetables — 60
pork: braised pork casserole — 26
    sweet and spicy pork — 28
potatoes: baby potato bites — 58

potato and celeriac soup — 12
potato wedges with a cooling dip, spicy — 58
potato-topped chilli beef — 29
prawn curry, stir-fry — 18
puddings: apple and ginger pudding — 46
    blackberry meringue pudding — 46
    creamy orange puddings — 42
    sticky toffee pudding — 45
pumpkin traybake, golden — 52

R

rice pudding crunch, apricot and almond — 40
risotto, tomato and basil — 32

S

sausages: campfire casserole — 56
    sausage and lentil casserole — 22
seafood stew, winter — 21
soufflés, hot banana — 42
soups: butterbean and broccoli soup — 13
    farmhouse chicken and vegetable broth — 9
    fisherman's catch — 10
    golden onion soup — 7
    harvest vegetable soup — 12
    potato and celeriac soup — 12
    red hot tomato and beetroot soup — 8
    spiced tomato, lentil and rice soup — 10
spinach, egg and cheese ramekins — 36
stews: chicken hotpot — 15
    Irish stew — 25
    winter seafood stew — 21
sticky toffee pudding — 45

T

tea bread, orchard fruit and ginger — 53
toffee: toffee apple wedges — 60
    toffee pudding, sticky — 45
tomatoes: aubergine, tomato and
    mozzarella bake — 31
    baked feta and tomato marrow — 35
    cheese, onion and tomato bread pudding — 32
    red hot tomato and beetroot soup — 8
    spiced tomato, lentil and rice soup — 10
    tomato and basil risotto — 32
turkey, parsnip and cheddar crumble — 18

V

vegetables: festive vegetable bourguignon — 36
    harvest vegetable soup — 12
    root vegetable bake — 34
    winter vegetable korma — 37

W

walnut pie, apple and — 47

Y

yogurt, yuletide — 57